American Textbook Reading

Science ❷

Table of Contents

Part 1   **Life Science**

Lesson 01   What Animals Need to Grow   10

Lesson 02   Living Things vs Nonliving Things   16

Lesson 03   Adaptations for Survival   22

Lesson 04   The Human Life Cycle   28

Part 2   **Earth Science**

Lesson 05   Weather   36

Lesson 06   Measuring the Weather   42

Lesson 07   Clouds and Rain   48

Lesson 08   Seasons   54

Lesson 09   The Sky   60

Part 3 — Physical Science

Lesson 10   Heat 68

Lesson 11   Light 74

Lesson 12   Sound 80

Lesson 13   Electricity 86

Lesson 14   Motion 92

Lesson 15   Magnets 98

Lesson Guide

Title
This is what the lesson is about.

Visual Summary
The visual summary uses images with key vocabulary and other related words to introduce the main concept of the lesson. The visual summary is also an aid for word association, reinforcing the meaning of the words within context.

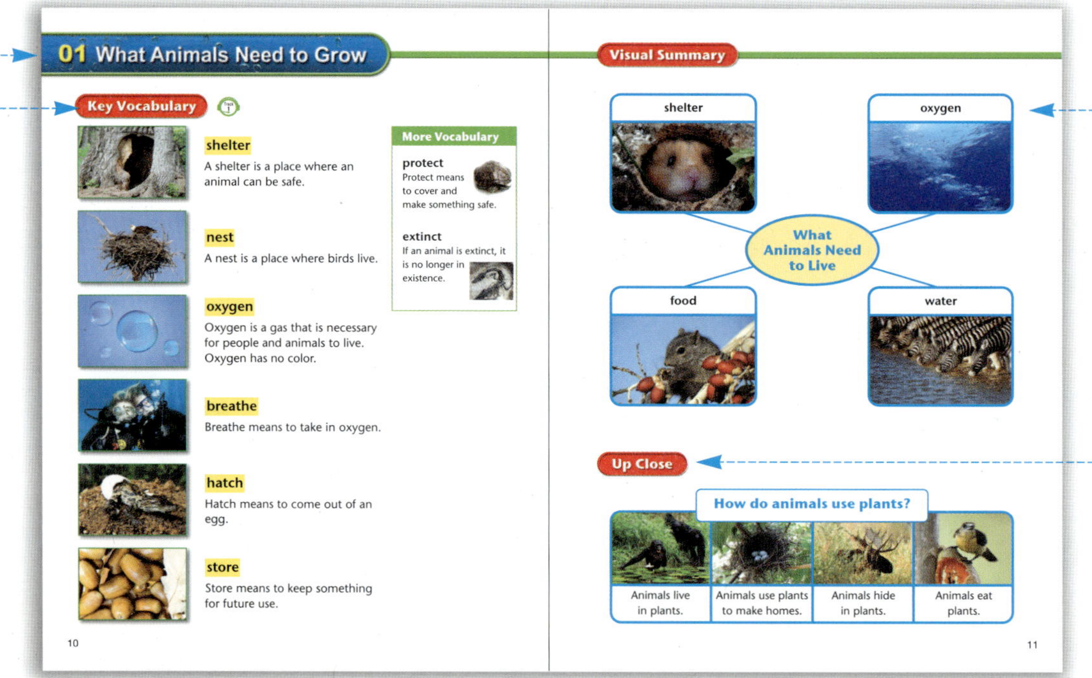

Key Vocabulary
These are new words for students to learn in the lesson.
The meaning of each word is below it.

Up Close
This expands the key vocabulary and the lesson's main idea. This gives students a greater level of understanding.

Review 1

Here there are pictures of objects or situations. Students can use a visual guide to help them remember a word.

Exercise

This exercise will test students' understanding of the written definition of the key vocabulary.

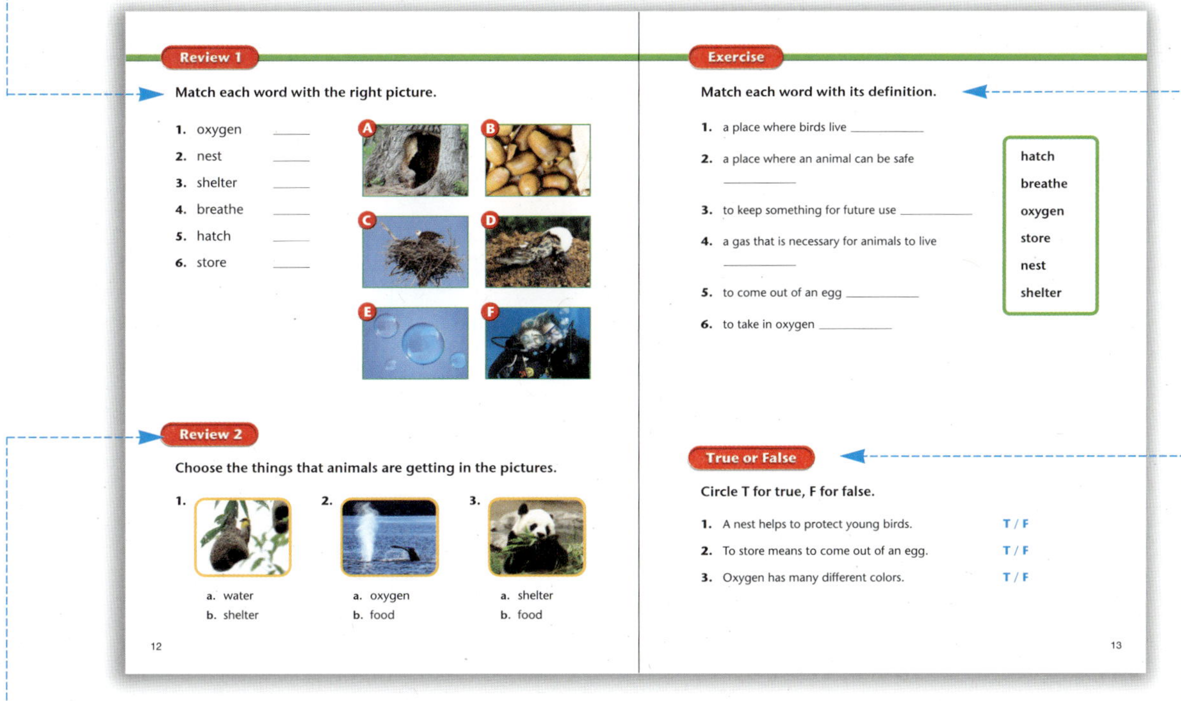

Review 2

Here there are new pictures that relate to the key vocabulary. Different pictures help students learn a new word and remember it.

True or False

This exercise make the students think carefully about a statement.

Reading

The passage is the main part of the lesson. It contains all the key vocabulary and other words students have been learning in this lesson. Students have been preparing for the passage in the previous pages. This makes it easier for students to comprehend the passage.

Comprehension

These questions test students' comprehension of the passage. They also test students' ability to remember what is written in the passage.

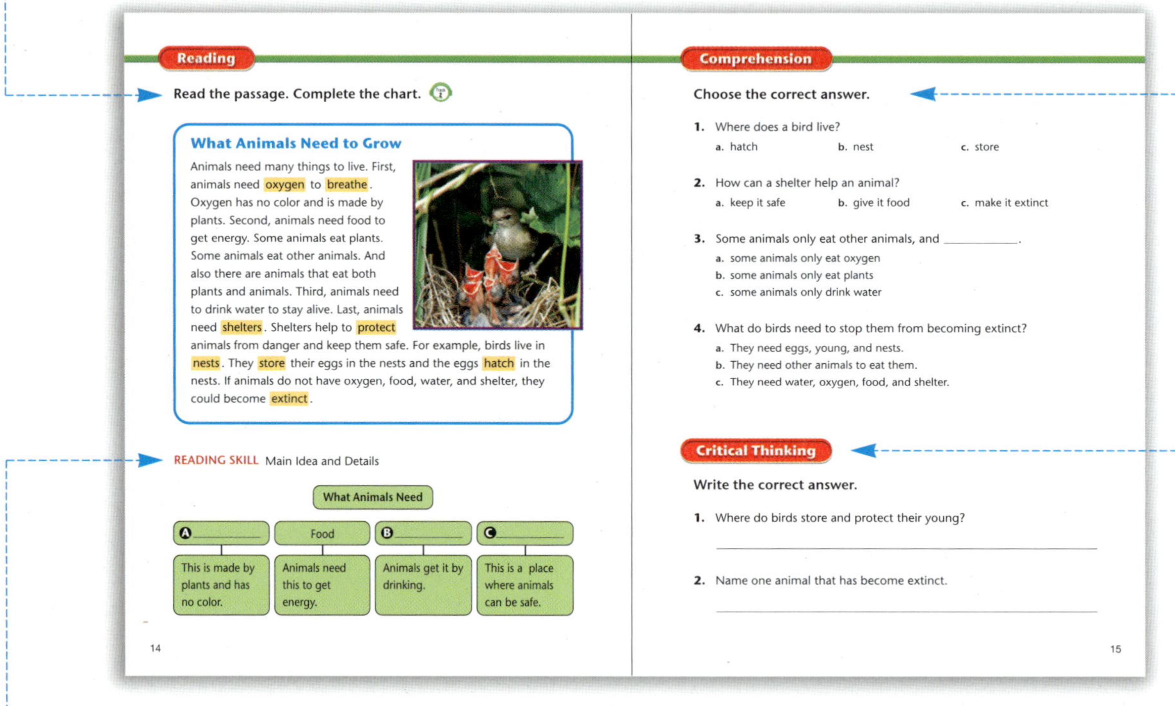

Reading Skill

Each passage follows a reading skill such as *Main Idea*, *Sequence*, *Compare* and *Contrast*, *Classify*, etc. The chart helps students identify and understand the key concepts or key parts of the passage. This aids comprehension.

Critical Thinking

These questions make students use critical thinking, which is an important part of the learning process. This section will help students develop their reading skills.

6

Vocabulary 1

These exercises test students' ability to remember the meaning of a word using a picture as a guide.

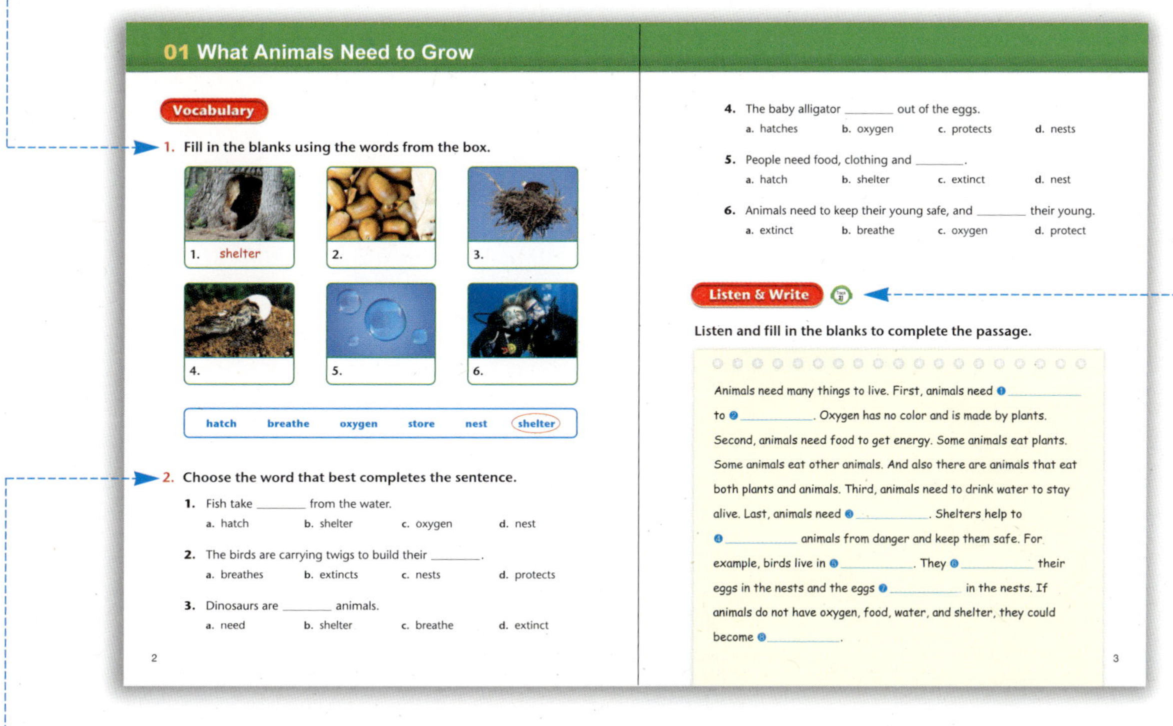

Vocabulary 2

These exercises make students use the key vocabulary words in a context that is different to that in the passage. This increases students' understanding and use of words.

Listen & Write

Students can practice their listening skills. A native speaker of English speaks the passage, and this allows students to hear the proper pronunciation of words.

Part 1
Life Science

Lesson 01 | **What Animals Need to Grow**

Lesson 02 | **Living Things vs Nonliving Things**

Lesson 03 | **Adaptations for Survival**

Lesson 04 | **The Human Life Cycle**

Key Vocabulary

ATR-SC2-01
MP3

shelter

A shelter is a place where an animal can be safe.

nest

A nest is a place where birds live.

oxygen

Oxygen is a gas that is necessary for people and animals to live. Oxygen has no color.

breathe

Breathe means to take in oxygen.

hatch

Hatch means to come out of an egg.

store

Store means to keep something for future use.

More Vocabulary

protect 
Protect means to cover and make something safe.

extinct
If an animal is extinct, it is no longer in existence. 

shelter

oxygen

What Animals Need to Live

food

water

Up Close

How do animals use plants?

| Animals live in plants. | Animals use plants to make homes. | Animals hide in plants. | Animals eat plants. |

Match each word with the right picture.

1. oxygen   ______
2. nest   ______
3. shelter   ______
4. breathe   ______
5. hatch   ______
6. store   ______

A 

B 

C 

D 

E

F

Choose the things that animals are getting in the pictures.

1. 
   a. water
   b. shelter

2. 
   a. oxygen
   b. food

3. 
   a. shelter
   b. food

Match each word with its definition.

1. a place where birds live _______________

2. a place where an animal can be safe

   ____

3. to keep something for future use _______________

4. a gas that is necessary for animals to live

   ____

5. to come out of an egg _______________

6. to take in oxygen _______________

hatch

breathe

oxygen

store

nest

shelter

Circle T for true, F for false.

1. A nest helps to protect young birds.　　　T / F

2. To store means to come out of an egg.　　　T / F

3. Oxygen has many different colors.　　　T / F

ATR-SC2-02
MP3

Read the passage. Complete the chart.

What Animals Need to Grow

Animals need many things to live. First, animals need oxygen to breathe. Oxygen has no color and is made by plants. Second, animals need food to get energy. Some animals eat plants. Some animals eat other animals. And also there are animals that eat both plants and animals. Third, animals need to drink water to stay alive. Last, animals need shelters. Shelters help to protect animals from danger and keep them safe. For example, birds live in nests. They store their eggs in the nests and the eggs hatch in the nests. If animals do not have oxygen, food, water, and shelter, they could become extinct.

READING SKILL Main Idea and Details

What Animals Need

A ___________	Food	B ___________	C ___________
This is made by plants and has no color.	Animals need this to get energy.	Animals get it by drinking.	This is a place where animals can be safe.

Choose the correct answer.

1. Where does a bird live?

    a. hatch   **b.** nest   **c.** store

2. How can a shelter help an animal?

    a. keep it safe   **b.** give it food   **c.** make it extinct

3. Some animals only eat other animals, and ______________.

    a. some animals only eat oxygen

    b. some animals only eat plants

    c. some animals only drink water

4. What do birds need to stop them from becoming extinct?

    a. They need eggs, young, and nests.

    b. They need other animals to eat them.

    c. They need water, oxygen, food, and shelter.

Critical Thinking

Write the correct answer.

1. Where do birds store and protect their young?

____

2. Name one animal that has become extinct.

____

Key Vocabulary

living things

Living things need water, air, and food to live. Animals and plants are living things.

nonliving things

Nonliving things do not need water, air, and food. Rocks and water are nonliving things.

environment

An environment is the place where a living thing lives.

survive

Survive means to continue living. A living thing needs water, air and food to survive.

grow

Grow means to get bigger. If you have food and water, you will grow.

rock

A rock is a small and hard nonliving thing.

More Vocabulary

nature
Nature is the world of living and nonliving things.

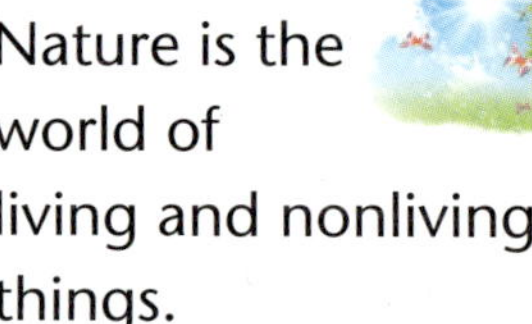

safe
If something is safe, there is no danger.

alive
Being alive means living, not dead.

The Differences between Living Things and Nonliving Things

living things	nonliving things

• alive • grow and change • need air, food, water, and space	• not alive • never grow • never need air, food, water

Up Close

living things					
	people	bird	rabbit	flowers	tree
nonliving things					
	rock	bike	clothes	car	book

Match each word with the right picture.

1. living things ______

2. nonliving things

______

3. environment ______

4. rock ______

5. survive ______

6. grow ______

Write L for living things and N for nonliving things.

1.

2.

3.

4.

______ ______ ______ ______

Match each word with its definition.

1. things that do not need water, air, or food

____

2. a small and hard nonliving thing

____

3. to continue living _________________

4. to get bigger _________________

5. the place where a living thing lives

____

6. things that need water, air, and food to live

____

> grow
>
> survive
>
> environment
>
> rock
>
> **living things**
>
> **nonliving things**

True or False

Circle T for true, F for false.

1. Nonliving things need food and water to survive.　　**T / F**

2. Living things grow and change.　　**T / F**

3. The environment is where living things live.　　**T / F**

ATR-SC2-04
MP3

Read the passage. Complete the chart.

Living Things vs Nonliving Things

Nature has many living and nonliving things in it. Living things need food and water to survive. Food and water help living things to grow and change. Mammals, reptiles, birds, insects, amphibians, and fish are living things. People are living things too. The place where a living thing lives is called its environment. A living thing must be safe in its environment. All living things are alive. Nonliving things are not alive. Nonliving things do not need food or water, and do not grow. Rocks and water are nonliving things.

READING SKILL Compare and Contrast

Nature has many living things and nonliving things in it.

Living Things

All living things are
A ____________.

They need **B** ____________ to survive.

They **C** ____________ and change.

Nonliving Things

Nonliving things are not
D ____________.

They don't need
E ____________ to survive.

They do not **F** ____________.

Choose the correct answer.

1. Nonliving things are not ______________.

    a. survive   **b.** alive   **c.** safe

2. What helps people to grow and survive?

    a. water and food   **b.** rocks and fish   **c.** an unsafe environment

3. Living things grow, but ______________.

    a. mammals and reptiles do not

    b. nonliving things do not

    c. the environment can never change

4. What does nature have in it?

    a. nonliving and living things

    b. only living things like mammals

    c. only nonliving things

Critical Thinking

Write the correct answer.

1. Name three living things and two nonliving things.

____

2. What does a living thing need to survive and help it grow?

____

Key Vocabulary

ATR-SC2-05
MP3

adaptation

An adaptation is a body part or a behavior that helps a living thing meet its needs.

shape
Shape is the outer form of something.

camouflage

Camouflage is the color or shape that helps an animal hide.

carnivore

A carnivore is an animal that only eats meat. A carnivore is at the top of the food chain.

herbivore

An herbivore is an animal that only eats plants. A rabbit is an herbivore.

wild

Being wild means living or growing in natural conditions.

spiny

Spiny means having sharp points like needles.

What do they eat?

| herbivores | 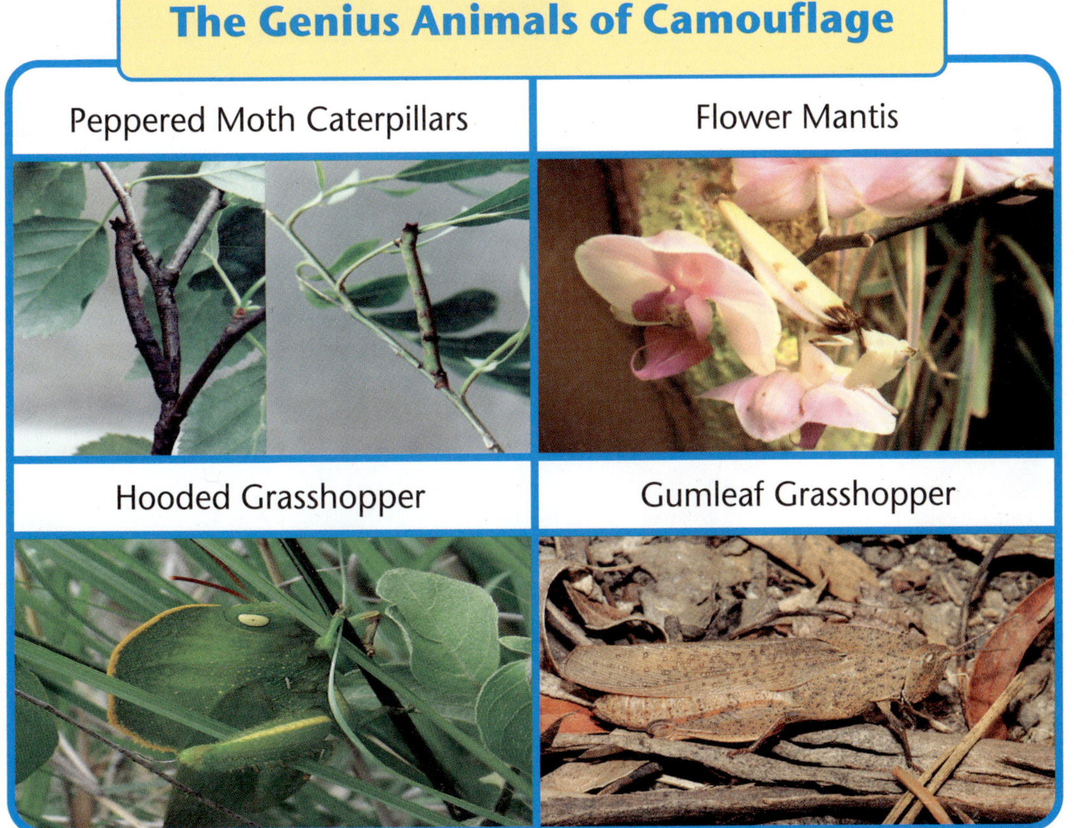 | - only eat plants
- have flat teeth
  (horse, squirrel, rabbit,
  etc.) |
| carnivores | | - eat other animals
- have sharp teeth
  (lion, tiger, shark, etc.) |

Up Close

The Genius Animals of Camouflage

| Peppered Moth Caterpillars | Flower Mantis |
| Hooded Grasshopper | Gumleaf Grasshopper |

Match each word with the right picture.

1. adaptation _______
2. spiny _______
3. camouflage _______
4. carnivore _______
5. herbivore _______
6. wild _______

A

B

C

D

E

F

Review 2

Choose the animal type for each picture.

1. 
   a. carnivore
   b. herbivore

2. 
   a. carnivore
   b. herbivore

3. 
   a. carnivore
   b. herbivore

4. 
   a. carnivore
   b. herbivore

Match each word with its definition.

1. having sharp points like needles _______________

2. an animal that only eats plants _______________

3. a body part that helps a living thing meet its needs _______________

4. an animal that only eats meat _______________

5. the color or shape of an animal that helps it hide _______________

6. living or growing in a natural habitat

   ____

> wild
>
> spiny
>
> adaptation
>
> herbivore
>
> camouflage
>
> carnivore

True or False

Circle T for true, F for false.

1. A carnivore is an animal that only eats plants.   T / F

2. An adaptation helps a nonliving thing.   T / F

3. Camouflage helps an animal hide.   T / F

ATR-SC2-06
MP3

Read the passage. Complete the chart.

Adaptations for Survival

Plants and animals have adaptations that help them survive.

An adaption is a body part or behavior that helps a living thing meet its need. For example, some animals have spikes all around their body which are very spiny so that they protect themselves from enemies. Wild animals have adaptations. Carnivores like tigers have sharp teeth for eating meat. Unlike carnivores, herbivores have flat teeth for eating plants. Camouflage is another adaptation. Camouflage is the color or shape of an animal that makes it blend in with its environment. A chameleon can change the color of its body so that it cannot be seen easily.

READING SKILL Compare and Contrast

Adaptation

ALIKE

It helps living things to
Ⓐ______________ and meet
their Ⓑ______________.

DIFFERENT

Some living things have
Ⓒ______________ spikes.

Some animals have special color or
Ⓓ______________ that help them hide.

Ⓔ______________ have sharp teeth.

Ⓕ______________ have flat teeth.

Comprehension

Choose the correct answer.

1. A chameleon can change what to help it hide?

   a. shape   **b.** color   **c.** spikes

2. Herbivores have _______________ for eating plants.

   a. flat teeth   **b.** spiny teeth   **c.** sharp teeth

3. How can an adaptation help an animal?

   a. by helping it eat and live

   b. by changing its environment

   c. by protecting it from camouflage

4. Herbivores do not eat meat, and _______________.

   a. carnivores only eat tigers and rabbits

   b. chameleons can change a plants color

   c. carnivores do not eat plants

Critical Thinking

Write the correct answer.

1. Name two carnivores and two herbivores.

   ____

2. What is a way to help an animal hide from its enemies?

   ____

Key Vocabulary

ATR-SC2-07
MP3

infant

An infant is a baby. An infant cannot walk or talk.

toddler

A toddler is a very young child. A toddler learns to walk and talk.

child

A child is a very young person who is no longer a baby but not yet a teen. A child goes to school.

teen

A teen is a person between the ages of 13 and 19. Teens are young adults.

adult

An adult is a fully grown person.

sleep

Sleep means to rest your body and mind with your eyes closed.

More Vocabulary

exercise
Exercise makes your body strong.

learn
When you study, you learn things.

Visual Summary

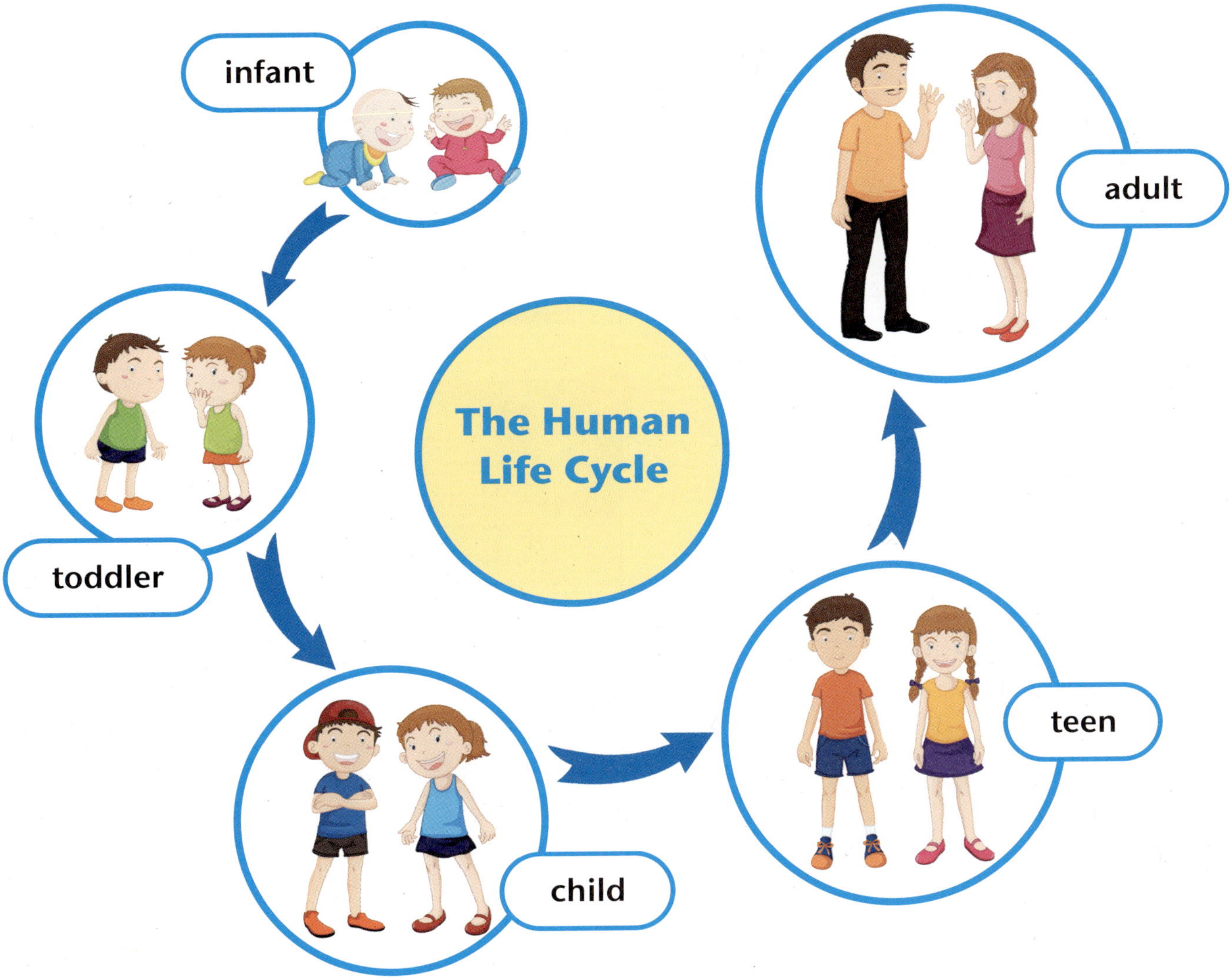

The Human Life Cycle
infant
toddler
child
teen
adult

Up Close

How to Stay Healthy

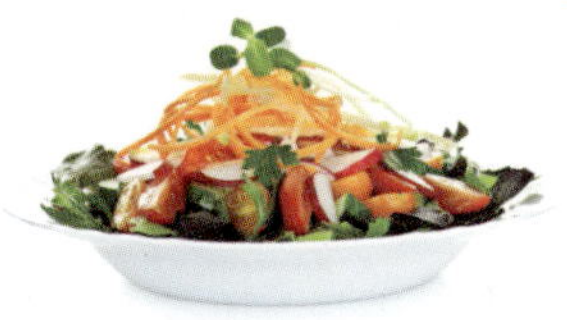

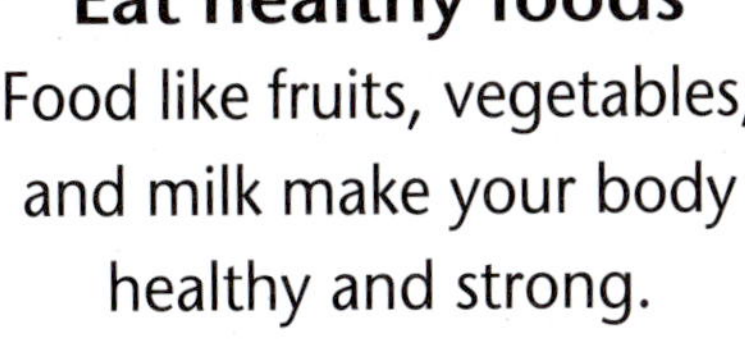

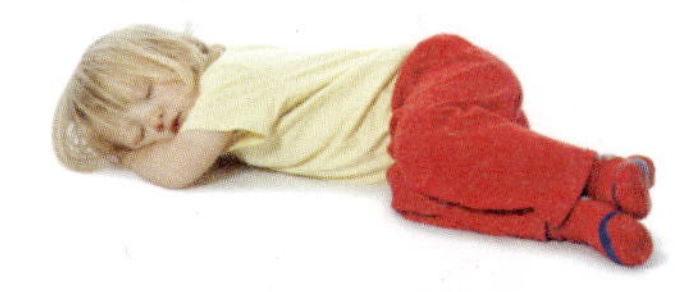

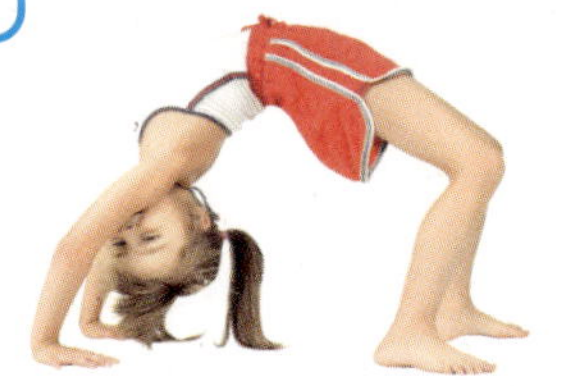

Eat healthy foods
Food like fruits, vegetables, and milk make your body healthy and strong.

Get enough sleep
You can rest your body and mind during sleep.

Do exercise
Running and jumping makes your body strong.

Match each word with the right picture.

1. sleep _______
2. infant _______
3. toddler _______
4. child _______
5. teen _______
6. adult _______

Circle unhealthy habits.

a. 

b. 

c. 

d. 

Match each word with its definition.

1. a baby who cannot walk or talk _______________

2. a fully grown person _______________

3. a very young person who is no longer a baby but not yet a teen _______________

4. a person between the ages of 13 and 19

   ____

5. to rest your body and mind with your eyes closed

   ____

6. a very young child who learns to walk and talk

   ____

> teen
>
> child
>
> infant
>
> adult
>
> sleep
>
> toddler

True or False

Circle T for true, F for false.

1. The first stage in the human life cycle is a toddler.　　T / F

2. An infant cannot walk or talk.　　T / F

3. A child is a person between 13 and 19 years old.　　T / F

ATR-SC2-08
MP3

Read the passage. Complete the chart.

The Human Life Cycle

The life cycle of people is amazing. A person starts very small as an infant. An infant cannot walk or talk. An infant grows into a toddler. A toddler starts to learn to walk and talk. A toddler will grow into a child. A child can walk and talk. Children begin to go to school and learn. When a person becomes 13 years old, we call them a teen. A teen is a person between 13 and 19 years old. When a person becomes over 19 years old, we call them an adult. An adult is a fully grown person. During this cycle, we should be healthy. What is important for being healthy? Every person should eat healthy foods and get enough sleep and exercise to be strong and healthy.

READING SKILL Sequence

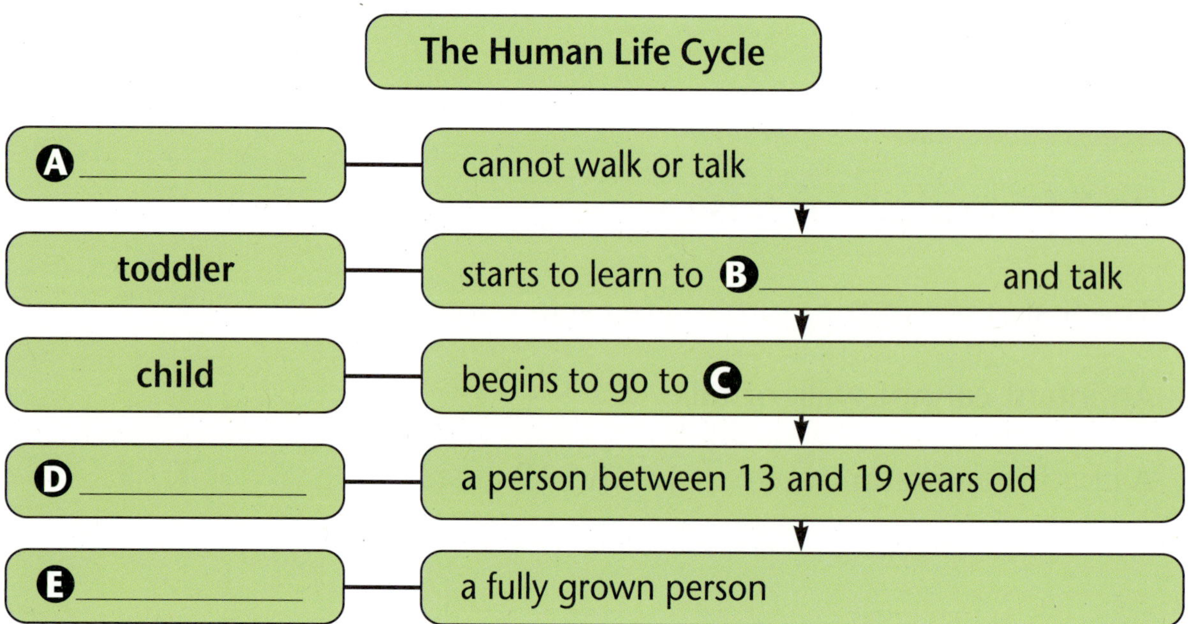

Choose the correct answer.

1. What does a teen become?

   a. toddler   **b.** child   **c.** adult

2. A child can walk and talk but is not yet ______________.

   a. fully grown   **b.** going to school   **c.** eating healthily

3. A teen is a person ______________.

   a. under 13 years old

   b. between 13 and 19 years old

   c. over 19 years old

4. What should people do to stay healthy?

   a. Eat vegetables and fruit, exercise and sleep well.

   b. Sleep a lot, eat healthy foods, but do not exercise.

   c. Go to school and learn to sleep.

Critical Thinking

Write the correct answer.

1. What is the first and last stage of the human life cycle?

____

2. Which stage are you in the human life cycle now?

____

Part 2
Earth Science

Lesson 05 | **Weather**

Lesson 06 | **Measuring the Weather**

Lesson 07 | **Clouds and Rain**

Lesson 08 | **Seasons**

Lesson 09 | **The Sky**

05 Weather

Key Vocabulary

ATR-SC2-09
MP3

weather

Weather is the conditions of the air outside relating to rain, snow, heat, cold, etc.

sunny

Sunny means with a lot of sunlight.

cloudy

Cloudy means to be covered with a lot of clouds.

windy

Windy means with a lot of wind.

rainy

Rainy means having a lot of rain.

snowy

Snowy means to be covered with snow.

More Vocabulary

sleet

Sleet is a mix of rain and snow.

observe

Observe means to see or watch something or somebody.

wet

Wet means to be covered with water.

Visual Summary

Types of Weather

cloudy

sunny

windy

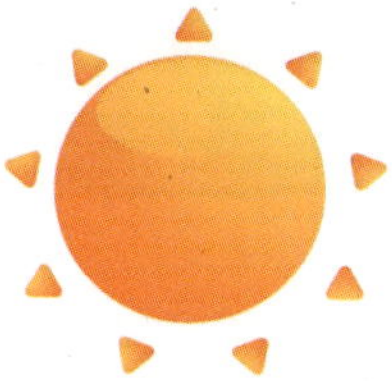

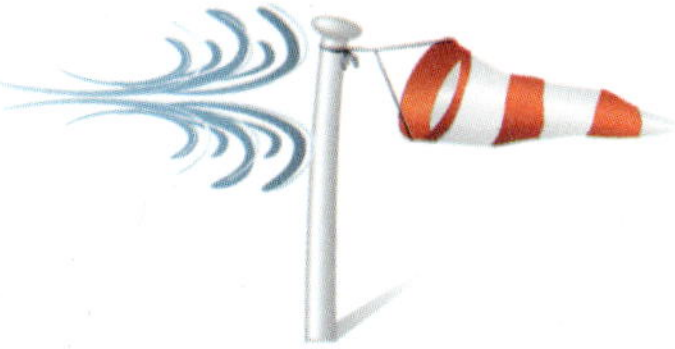

foggy

snowy

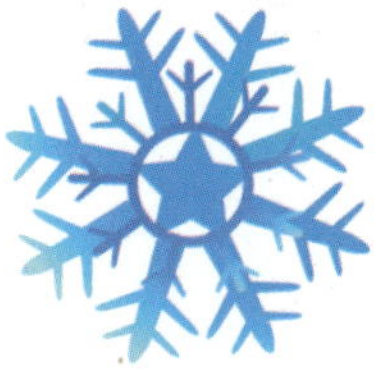

rainy

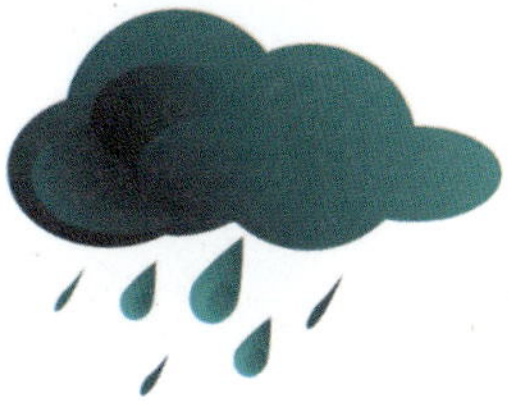

Up Close

Types of Wet Weather

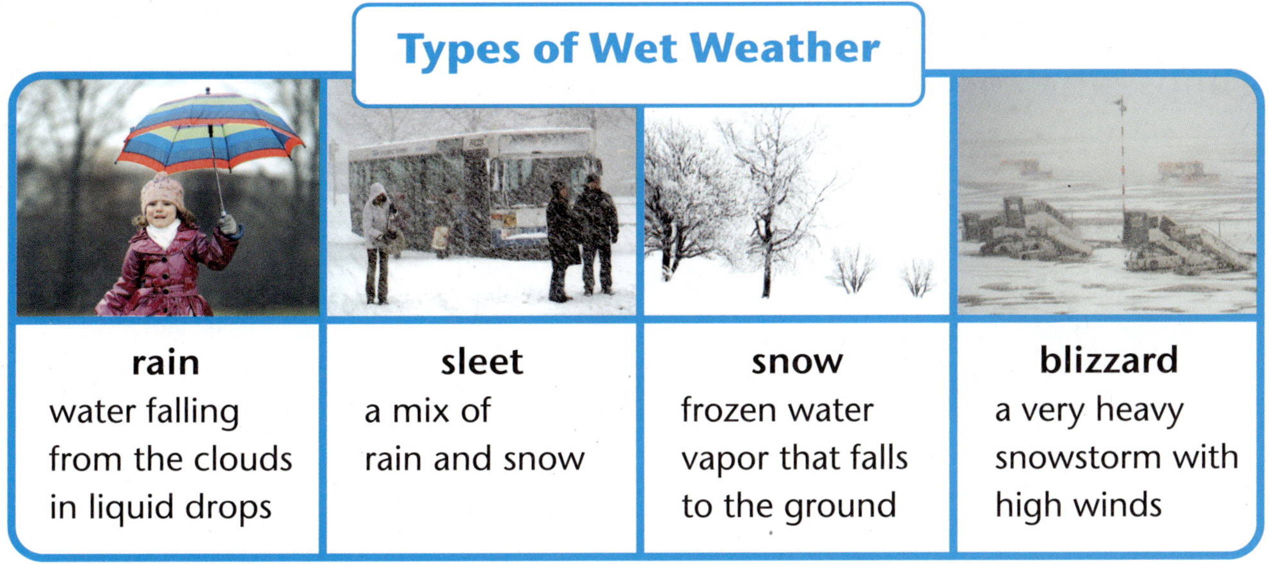

rain
water falling from the clouds in liquid drops

sleet
a mix of rain and snow

snow
frozen water vapor that falls to the ground

blizzard
a very heavy snowstorm with high winds

Match each word with the right picture.

1. snowy   _______
2. windy   _______
3. rainy   _______
4. cloudy   _______
5. sunny   _______
6. weather   _______

A

B

C

D

E

F

Choose the correct answer for each picture.

1. 

2. 

a. It is foggy.
b. It is sunny.
c. It is windy.
d. It is snowy.

____________   ____________

Match each word with its definition.

1. with a lot of wind ________________

2. to be covered with a lot of clouds

____

3. with a lot of sunlight ________________

4. having a lot of rain ________________

5. the conditions of the air outside relating to
rain, snow, heat, cold, etc. ________________

6. to be covered with snow ________________

> sunny
>
> rainy
>
> windy
>
> weather
>
> cloudy
>
> snowy

True or False

Circle T for true, F for false.

1. Sleet is a mix of snow and rain.   **T / F**

2. On a cloudy day, there is a lot of sunlight.   **T / F**

3. Weather never changes.   **T / F**

ATR-SC2-10
MP3

Read the passage. Complete the chart.

Weather

Weather is the conditions of the air outside. There are many different kinds of weather. It can be warm, cool, hot, or cold. You can **observe** how weather changes. Sometimes there is **snowy** weather. On snowy days, the weather is very cold. Sometimes there is **sleet**. Sleet is a mix of snow and rain. On **rainy** days, the weather is **wet**. The rainy season occurs between June and July in some places. On **windy** days, you have to be careful of the wind. It might blow you away! When the weather is **cloudy**, it could mean rain is coming. Sometimes the weather is beautiful and there is a lot of sun. This is called **sunny** weather. It is good for people to play outside.

READING SKILL Compare and Contrast

ALIKE

All weather is the conditions of the Ⓐ______________ outside.

You can observe how weather Ⓒ______________.

DIFFERENT

It can be warm, cool, hot, or Ⓑ______________.

It can be snowy, rainy, windy, Ⓓ______________, or sunny.

Choose the correct answer.

1. What is the weather like when it is rainy?

   a. dry **b.** season **c.** wet

2. On a snowy day, the weather is very _______________.

   a. cold **b.** hot **c.** warm

3. When it gets more and more cloudy, _______________.

   a. rain or snow might fall
   b. the rainy season will stop
   c. it is the best time to play outside

4. On a very windy day, _______________.

   a. the weather doesn't change
   b. sleet or snow can never fall
   c. the wind might blow you away

Critical Thinking

Write the correct answer.

1. What is the best kind of weather for playing outside?

   ____

2. What is the weather like in winter? What is the weather like in summer?

   ____

Key Vocabulary

ATR-SC2-11
MP3

measure

Measure means to find the size, speed, or amount of something using a tool.

blow

Blow means to move air through space.

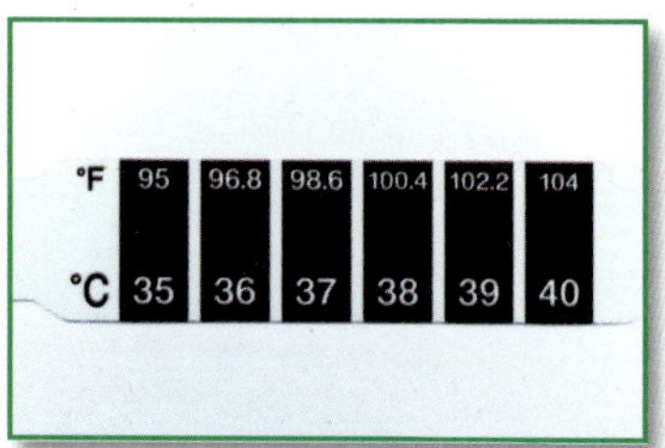

temperature

Temperature is how warm or cool something is.

thermometer

A thermometer is a tool used to measure the temperature.

rain gauge

A rain gauge is a tool used to measure how much rain has fallen.

wind vane

A wind vane is a tool used to measure the direction the wind is blowing.

direction

A direction is the path of something.

Measuring the Weather		
thermometer		measures how hot or cold something is
wind vane		measures the direction of the wind
rain gauge		measures how much rain has fallen

Up Close

Who studies the weather?

A meteorologist is a scientist who studies the weather.
Meteorologists tell us what the weather will be like tomorrow.

Match each word with the right picture.

1. temperature ______
2. thermometer ______
3. rain gauge ______
4. wind vane ______
5. measure ______
6. direction ______

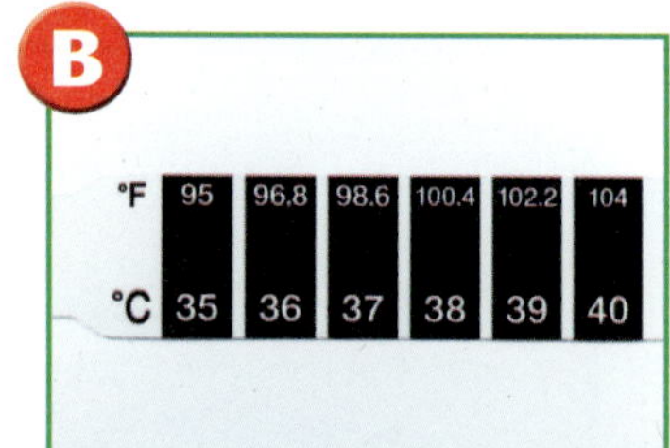

Choose what the tool in each picture measures.

1. 

   a. wind direction
   b. rainfall

2. 

   a. rainfall
   b. wind speed

3. 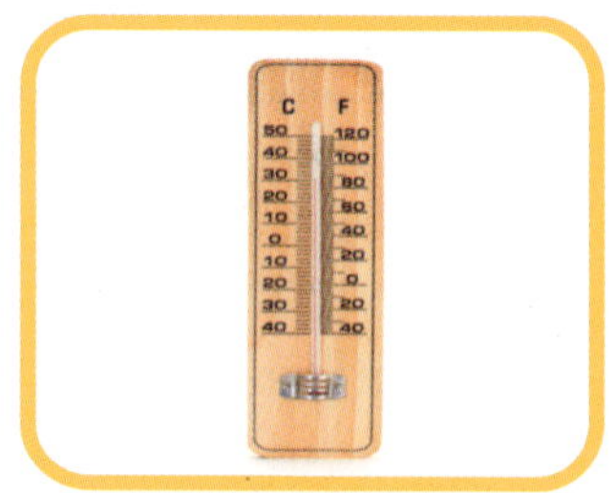

   a. wind direction
   b. temperature

Match each word with its definition.

1. a tool used to measure temperature

   ____

2. how warm or cool something is

   ____

3. a tool used to measure the direction the
   wind is blowing _______________

4. a tool used to measure how much rain has
   fallen _______________

5. to find the size, speed, or amount of
   something using a tool _______________

6. the path of something _______________

> direction
>
> thermometer
>
> rain gauge
>
> wind vane
>
> measure
>
> temperature

Circle T for true, F for false.

1. People use a thermometer to measure the temperature   **T / F**
   of the air.

2. People use a wind vane to measure the speed of wind.   **T / F**

3. A rain gauge can be used to measure which direction   **T / F**
   the wind is blowing.

Read the passage. Complete the chart.

Measuring the Weather

People can use tools to **measure** weather. Weather can be measured in many ways. One way to measure is to find the **temperature** of the air. Temperature is the measure of how hot or cold something is. People can use a **thermometer** to measure the temperature of the air. People can

also measure how much rain has fallen. A **rain gauge** can be used to measure the amount of rain that has fallen. We can measure the direction and speed of wind. The **direction** the wind is **blowing** can be measured by a **wind vane** . A thermometer, rain gauge, and wind vane are all tools used to measure weather.

READING SKILL Main Idea and Details

Weather can be measured in many ways.

A______ is the measure of how hot or cold something is. A(n) B______ is a tool for measuring it.	We can measure how much rain has fallen. A(n) C______ is used for this.	The direction of wind can be measured by a(n) D______.

Choose the correct answer.

1. A meteorologist is someone who studies the ______________.

    a. people   **b.** weather   **c.** tools

2. Temperature is the measure of how ______________ something is.

    a. warm or cool   **b.** wet   **c.** fast

3. A rain gauge can measure how much rain has fallen, ______________.

    a. but it cannot measure temperature

    b. and it can also measure wind direction

    c. and measures the same as a thermometer

4. Some tools used to measure the weather are ______________.

    a. a meteorologist and a scientist

    b. a wind vane and a thermometer

    c. rainfall, temperature, and wind speed

Critical Thinking

Write the correct answer.

1. Name three tools used to measure the weather.

    ____

2. You want to know if it will rain tomorrow. Who is the best person to ask?

    ____

Key Vocabulary

ATR-SC2-13
MP3

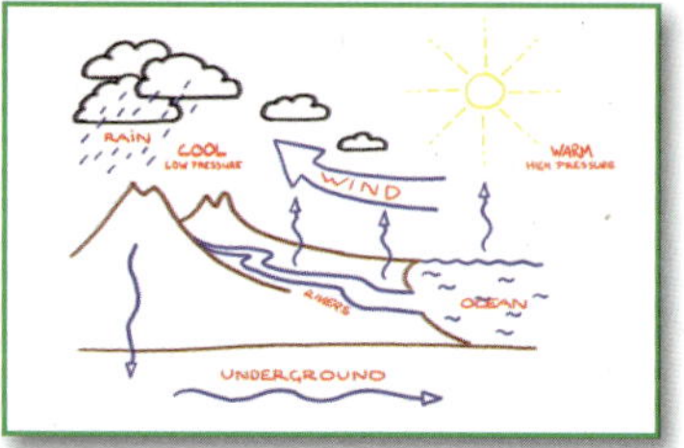

cycle

A cycle is a series of events being repeated many times.

cloud

A cloud is many drops of water that are together in the sky.

evaporate

Evaporate means to change from water to water vapor.

condense

Condense means to change from water vapor to water drops.

water vapor

Water vapor is the water that goes up into the air as a gas.

drop

A drop is a small amount of water.

Visual Summary

Water Cycle
2 As water vapor cools in the sky, it changes into tiny water drops. The drops form clouds.
3 When the water drops get bigger and bigger, they fall as rain or snow.
1 As the Sun warms water, some water turns into water vapor. Water vapor goes up into the air.

Up Close

Telling Weather by Looking at Clouds

thin and feathery clouds
a sign of good weather

puffy and white clouds
a sign of good weather

low and gray clouds
a sign of stormy weather

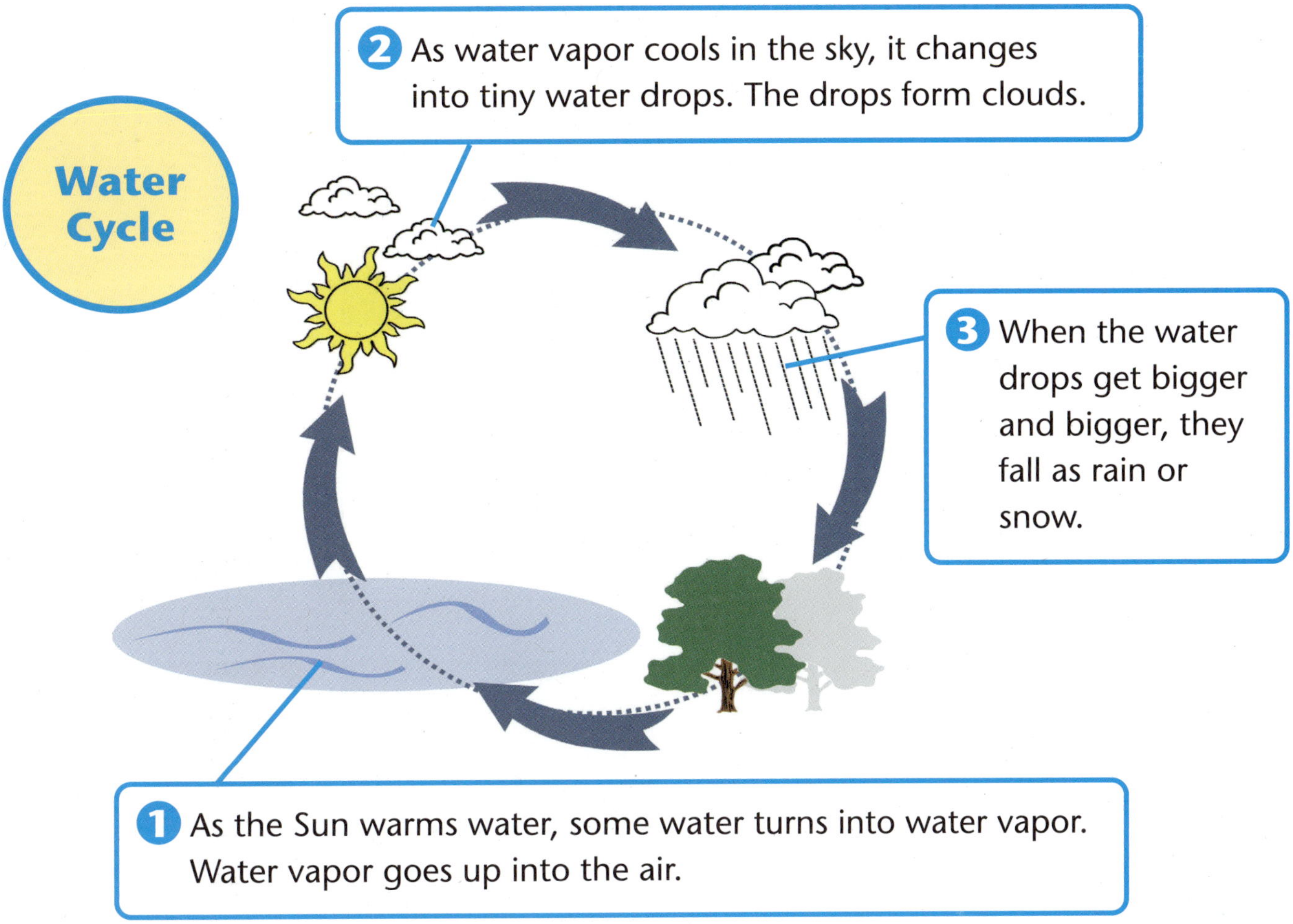

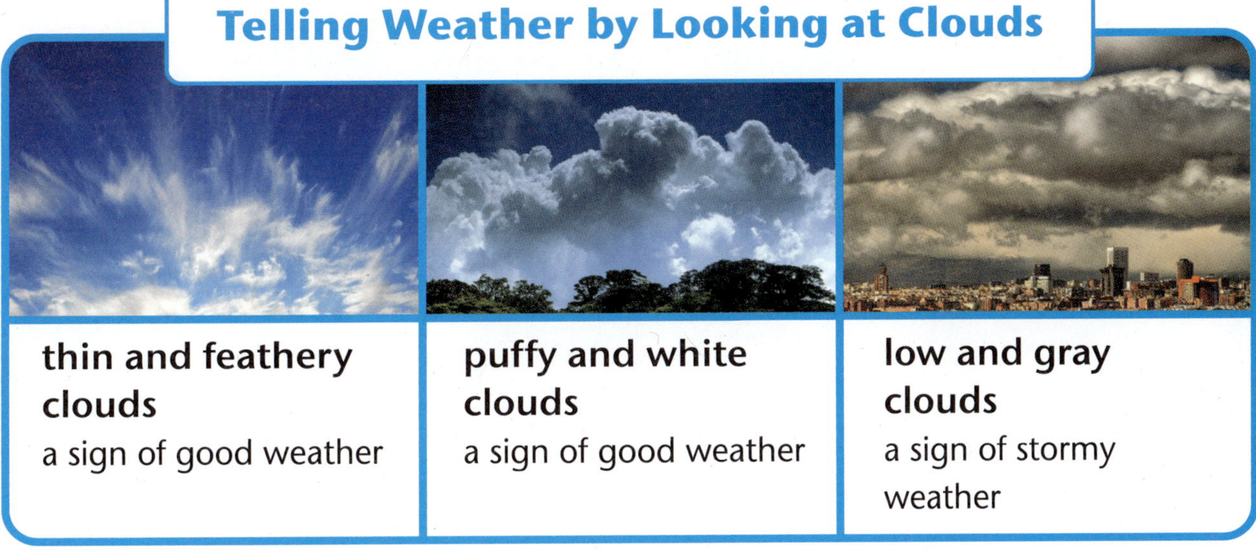

Match each word with the right picture.

1. cycle ______
2. drop ______
3. condense ______
4. water vapor ______
5. cloud ______
6. evaporate ______

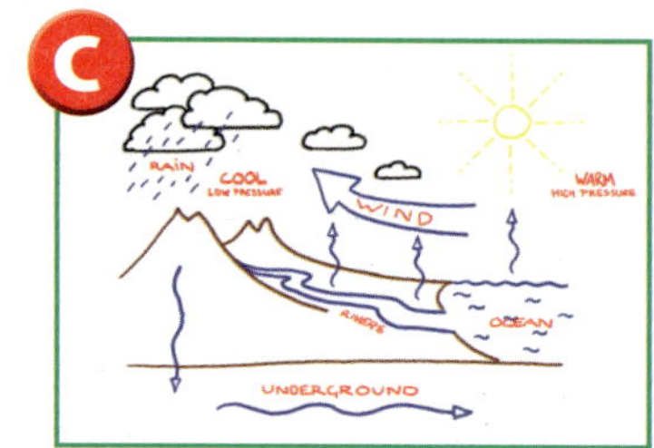

Review 2

Circle the pictures that show signs of good weather.

1.

2.

3.

Match each word with its definition.

1. a series of events being repeated many times

   ____

2. a small amount of water _______________

3. the many drops of water together in the sky

   ____

4. to change from water to water vapor

   ____

5. to change from water vapor to water drops

   ____

6. the water that goes up into the air as a gas

   ____

> cycle
>
> drop
>
> condense
>
> water vapor
>
> cloud
>
> evaporate

True or False

Circle T for true, F for false.

1. Water vapor is the water that goes up into the air as a gas. T / F

2. Evaporate means to change from water vapor to water. T / F

3. Condense means to change from water to water vapor. T / F

ATR-SC2-14
MP3

Read the passage. Complete the chart.

Clouds and Rain

Water moves from place to place. Water moves from the earth to the air and back again. This is called the water cycle. The Sun makes water warm. Then the water evaporates, or changes into water vapor. We cannot see water vapor. Water vapor goes up into the air. Water vapor cools in the sky. Then water vapor condenses, or changes into tiny water drops. Many drops of water form clouds. Water drops in the clouds get bigger and bigger. They then fall back to the earth as rain or snow. The rain or snow falls into rivers, lakes and oceans. And the water cycle continues.

READING SKILL Cause and Effect

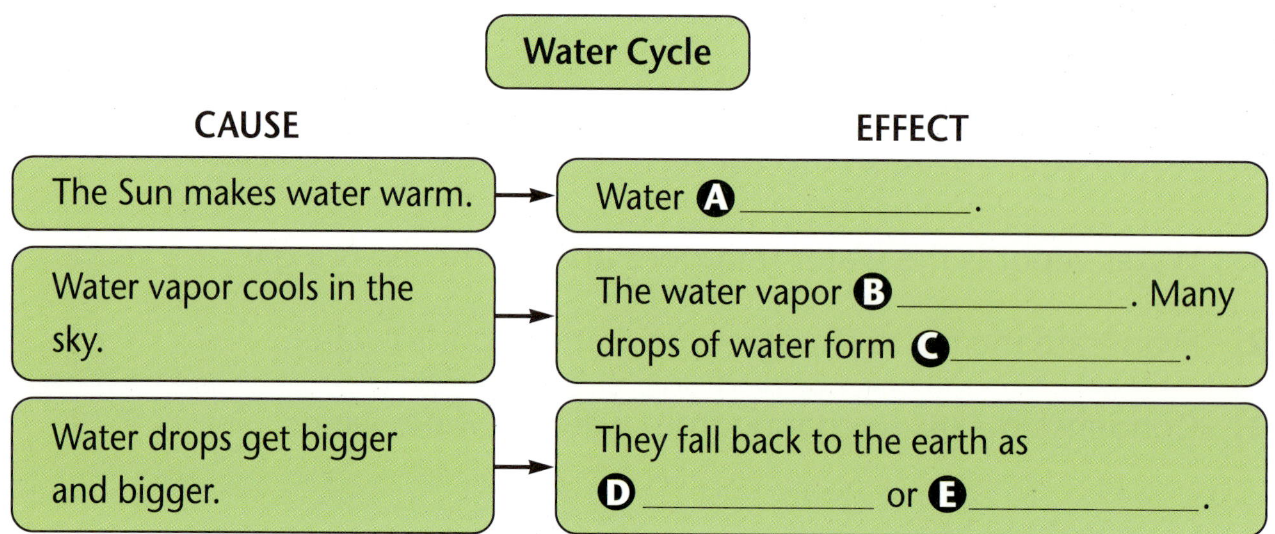

Choose the correct answer.

1. The sun warms water, and next the water ______________.

    a. rains   **b.** evaporates   **c.** cycles

2. Rain or snow falls into ______________.

    a. the earth as vapor   **b.** lakes and rivers   **c.** clouds and the Sun

3. The water cycle is when water ______________.

    a. moves from the earth to the Sun

    b. condenses and goes up into the air

    c. moves from place to place

4. After water is warmed by the Sun, it can ______________.

    a. condense, and then fall as rain

    b. become water vapor in lakes and oceans

    c. condense, then evaporate, and then fall as snow

Critical Thinking

Write the correct answer.

1. Explain how some water turns into water vapor.

2. Explain how water drops form clouds.

Key Vocabulary

ATR-SC2-15
MP3

season

A season is any of the four main periods of the year.

spring

Spring is the season between winter and summer.

summer

Summer is the warmest season of the year. It comes after spring.

fall

Fall is the season between summer and winter.

winter

Winter is the coldest season of the year. It comes after fall.

daylight

Daylight is the light that comes from the sun during the day.

More Vocabulary

similar

Similar means almost alike.

pattern

A pattern is something that happens in a cycle.

ripe

If something is ripe, it is ready to eat.

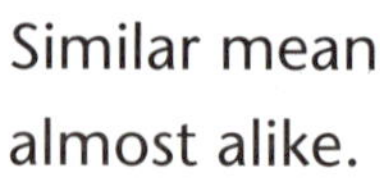

Four Seasons

spring		The weather gets warm. People go outside. Plants begin to grow.
summer		The weather gets hot. People wear light clothes. Plants grow fruits.
fall		The weather gets cool. People wear heavier clothes. Leaves change color and drop from trees.
winter		The weather gets cold. People wear very heavy clothes. Some plants have no leaves.

Up Close

The Seasons and the Sun

Date	Sunrise	Sunset	Daylight Hours
March 25	6:07 AM	6:15 PM	12 Hours, 8 Minutes
July 25	5:35 AM	8:19 PM	14 Hours, 44 Minutes
September 25	6:51 AM	7:00 PM	12 Hours, 9 Minutes
December 25	7:15 AM	5:56 PM	10 Hours, 41 Minutes

Match each word with the right picture.

1. spring   ______

2. summer   ______

3. fall   ______

4. winter   ______

5. daylight   ______

6. season   ______

Choose the season with longer hours of daylight.

1.

a. spring   **b.** summer

2.

a. fall   **b.** winter

Match each word with its definition.

1. the season between summer and winter

____

2. the season between winter and summer

____

3. the light that comes from the sun during the

day _______________

4. any of the four main periods of the year

____

5. the coldest season of the year and coming after

fall _______________

6. the warmest season of the year and coming after

spring _______________

spring

summer

fall

winter

daylight

season

True or False

Circle T for true, F for false.

1. Winter is a warm and colorful season.   **T / F**

2. In summer, there is little daylight.   **T / F**

3. The pattern of the seasons is always the same.   **T / F**

ATR-SC2-16
MP3

Read the passage. Complete the chart.

Seasons

A season is a time of year. There are four different seasons. Every season has different weather. The pattern of the seasons is always the same every year. Spring is a warm and colorful season. There are many hours of daylight in spring. We can play outside and enjoy the plant blossoms. In summer, the weather is similar to spring but it becomes much hotter. Summer is a season for swimming at the beach. The weather becomes colder in fall. There are less hours of daylight than in summer. Leaves change colors and drop from trees. Many fruits and vegetables are ripe in fall. Winter is the coldest season. In winter, snow falls and we have to wear our hats and gloves. Every season is different. There are special things to do in every season.

READING SKILL Main Idea and Details

There are four different seasons.

Spring is a(n) **A**__________ and colorful season. There are many hours of **B**__________.

In summer, the weather is much **C**__________ than spring.

In fall, many fruits and vegetables are **D**__________.

Winter is the **E**__________ season. Snow falls and we wear hats and gloves.

Choose the correct answer.

1. Spring is the season that comes after ______________.
   a. summer   b. fall   c. winter

2. Many fruits are ripe ______________.
   a. in winter   b. in spring   c. in fall

3. The hours of daylight in spring ______________.
   a. are more than that in winter
   b. make spring the best for swimming
   c. are less than that in winter

4. The pattern of the seasons is from ______________.
   a. summer to fall, and then spring to winter
   b. spring to fall, and then summer to winter
   c. winter to spring, and then summer to fall

Critical Thinking

Write the correct answer.

1. Which season is the best to see plants blossom?

   ____

2. In what season do leaves change color and drop from trees?

   ____

Key Vocabulary

ATR-SC2-17
MP3

star

A star is a bright object in the sky that makes its own light.

sun

The Sun is the star closest to the Earth. The Sun gives us light and warmth.

moon

The moon is the round object that moves around the Earth.

planet

A planet is an object that moves around the Sun.

rotate

Rotate means to spin. Day and night happen when the Earth rotates.

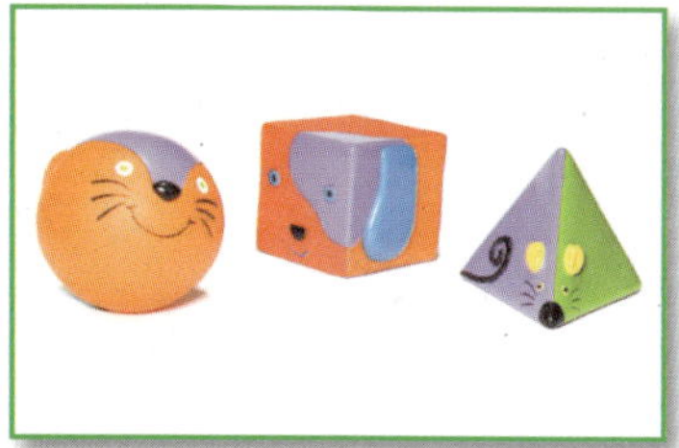

object

An object is a thing that we can see and touch.

Visual Summary

The Sky Above		
the Sun	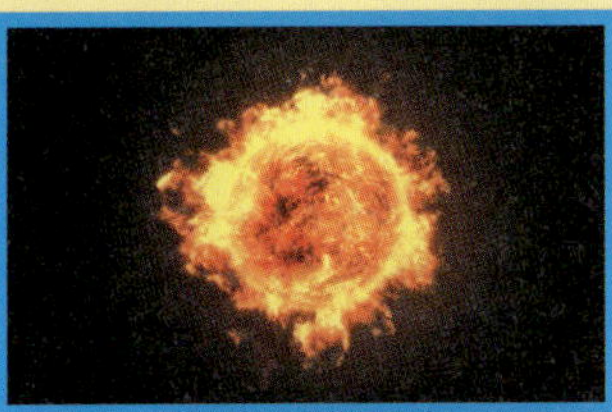	- the brightest object in the sky - the star closest to Earth
the moon	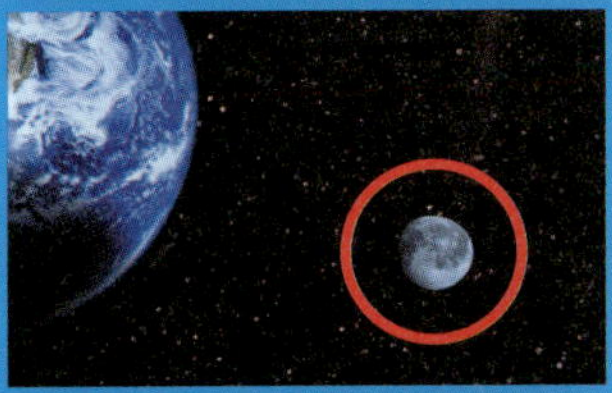	- a ball of rock that moves around the Earth
stars	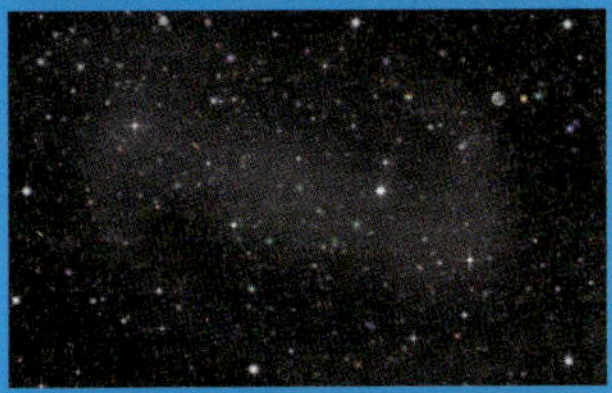	- objects in the sky that make their own light
planet	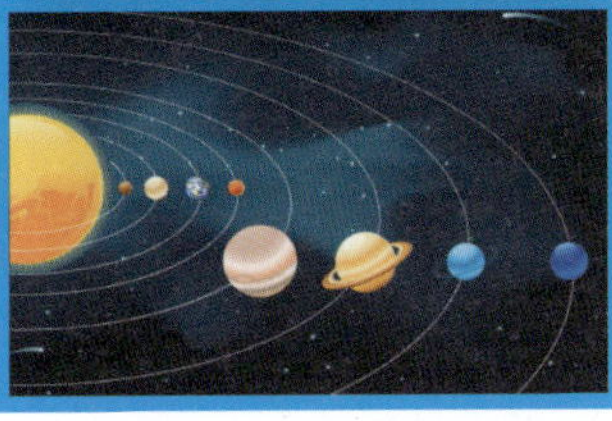	- a very large object that moves around the Sun

Up Close

What causes day and night?

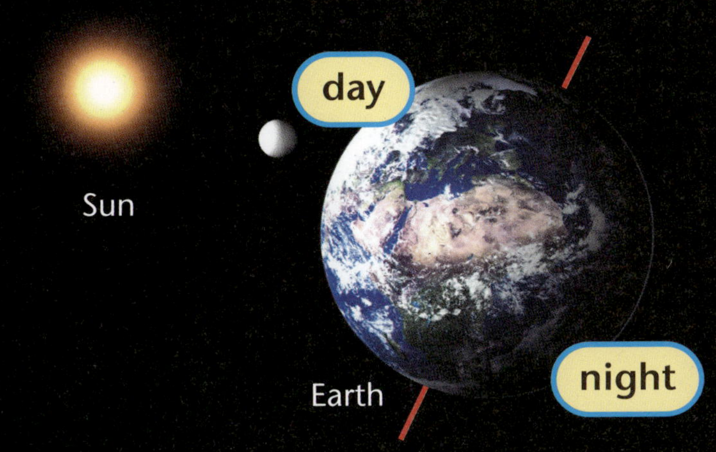

The sun shines on different sides of Earth as it rotates.

Match each word with the right picture.

1. sun _______
2. star _______
3. moon _______
4. planet _______
5. rotate _______
6. object _______

A

B

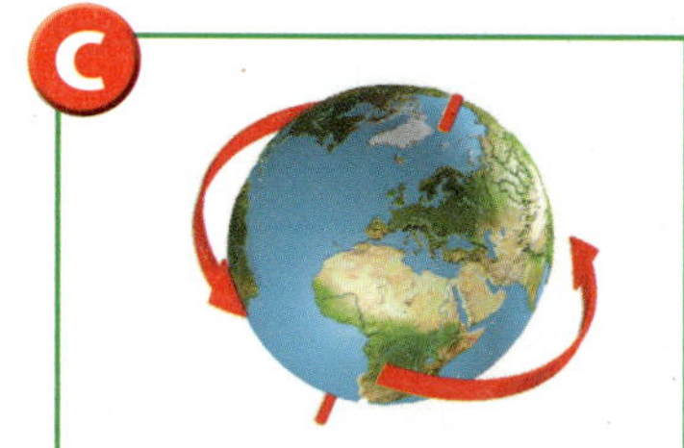
C

D

E

F

Write a or b for each picture.

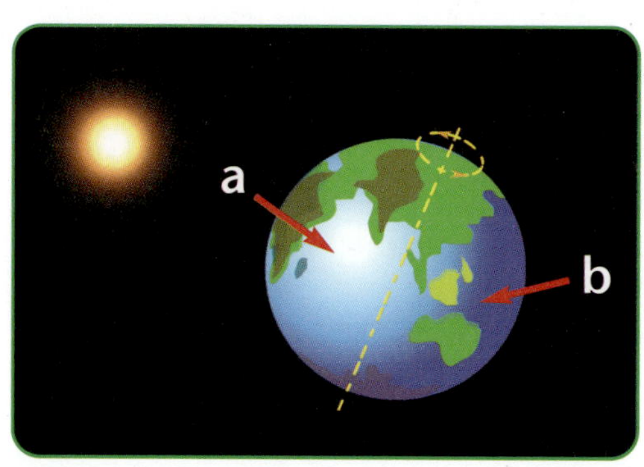

1.

2.

_______   _______

Match each word with its definition.

1. a thing that we can see and touch _______________

2. the round object that moves around the Earth

____

3. the star closest to the Earth that gives us light and warmth _______________

4. a bright object in the sky that makes its own light

____

5. to spin _______________

6. an object which moves around the Sun

____

sun

star

moon

planet

rotate

object

True or False

Circle T for true, F for false.

1. Stars are bright objects that move around the earth.　　T / F

2. The Sun is the planet closest to the Earth.　　T / F

3. Planets move around the Sun.　　T / F

ATR-SC2-18
MP3

Read the passage. Complete the chart.

The Sky

Every day, the Sun looks like it is moving across the sky. But actually the Sun is not moving. The Sun looks like it is moving as the Earth rotates. When the side we live on faces the Sun, we have day. When the side we live on turns away from the Sun, we have night. In the day sky, we can see the Sun. The Sun is a star. A star is an object that makes its own light. The Sun gives light and warmth to the Earth. There's no sunlight in the night sky. In night sky we can see planets, stars and the moon. Planets are objects that move around the Sun. The Earth is a planet. The moon is the object that moves around the Earth. Planets, stars and the moon look small because they are far away from the Earth.

READING SKILL Main Idea and Details

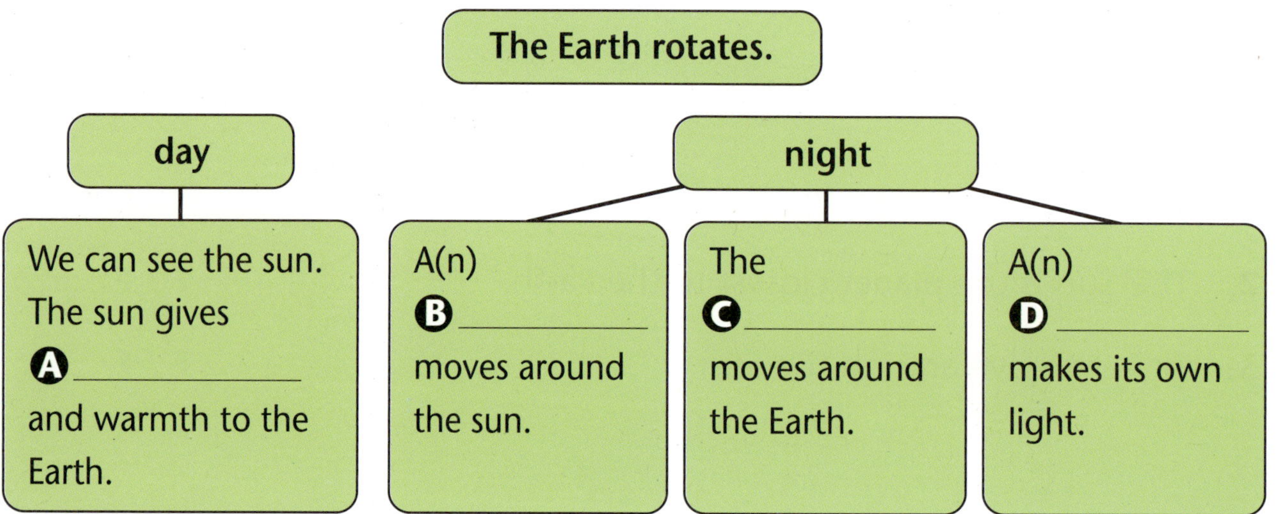

Choose the correct answer.

1. In the night sky, you cannot see the ______________.

   a. Sun
   b. moon
   c. planets

2. What is the planet we live on that moves around the Sun?

   a. the Earth
   b. the moon
   c. the star

3. The moon and planets look small because ______________.

   a. they are close to the Sun
   b. they are bigger than the stars
   c. they are far away from the Earth

4. The side of the Earth that is facing the Sun ______________.

   a. has both day and night because of the Sun
   b. has night and you cannot see the Sun
   c. has day and you can see the Sun

Critical Thinking

Write the correct answer.

1. Why is the Sun important for us?

   ____

2. What can you see in the night sky?

   ____

Part 3
Physical Science

Lesson 10 | **Heat**

Lesson 11 | **Light**

Lesson 12 | **Sound**

Lesson 13 | **Electricity**

Lesson 14 | **Motion**

Lesson 15 | **Magnets**

10 Heat

ATR-SC2-19
MP3

heat

Heat is a kind of energy that makes things hot.

energy

Energy is power that makes things work or causes change.

warm

Warm means to make something hot.

rub

Rub means to move two things together quickly.

stove

A stove is a piece of kitchen equipment that cooks food using heat.

lamp

A lamp is a device that uses electricity to produce light.

sun

fire

Heat Sources

light

rubbing hands

Up Close

Heat changes things.

Heat makes ice melt.

Heat cooks food.

Heat makes metal melt.

Match each word with the right picture.

1. energy _______

2. warm _______

3. rub _______

4. heat _______

5. lamp _______

6. stove _______

Review 2

Choose the thing or things which can be melted by heat.

a.

b.

c.

Match each word with its definition.

1. a device that uses electricity to produce light

   ____

2. to move two things together quickly ______________

3. to make something hot ______________

4. a piece of kitchen equipment that cooks food
   using heat ______________

5. power that makes things work or causes changes

   ____

6. a kind of energy that makes things hot

   ____

energy

warm

rub

heat

lamp

stove

True or False

Circle T for true, F for false.

1. Heat is energy that makes things cold. **T / F**

2. When you rub your hands, you move your hands together. **T / F**

3. A stove is a device that produces electricity. **T / F**

Read the passage. Complete the chart.

Heat

Heat is a kind of energy. Heat, light, sound and electricity are forms of energy. Energy is something that makes things work or causes changes. Heat comes from many things. The Sun warms the Earth's land, water, and air. We get heat from burning things like wood or gas. Lamps produce light and also make heat. Rubbing your hands together warms your hands. Heat is an important energy for us. Heat makes ice melt. Heat warms our body and our homes in winter. We also use heat to cook. We can cook food on a stove.

READING SKILL Main Idea and Details

Heat is a kind of **A** _____________ .

B _____________ warms the Earth's land, water, and air.

We get heat from **C** _____________ things like wood or gas.

D _____________ produce light and also make heat.

E _____________ your hands together warms your hands.

Choose the correct answer.

1. What do we use to make light?

    a. ice   **b.** lamps   **c.** sounds

2. What can heat do to metal and ice?

    a. make them melt   **b.** make them burn   **c.** make them cook

3. How do we usually warm our homes?

    a. by melting ice on the stove
    b. by burning things like wood or gas
    c. by rubbing our hands together quickly

4. Heat comes from many things, such as ______________.

    a. sound, light, and electricity
    b. burning things and the Sun
    c. ice, lamps, and the Sun

Critical Thinking

Write the correct answer.

1. What is the energy that makes things warm?

____

2. Where does the energy come from that warms the Earth's land, water, and air?

____

11 Light

Key Vocabulary

ATR-SC2-21
MP3

light

Light is the energy that makes it possible to see things.

dark

Dark means with no or very little light.

shadow

A shadow is the dark place made when an object blocks light.

streetlight

A streetlight is a lamp on the street.

pass

Pass means to go through.

sunglasses

Sunglasses are dark glasses that protect your eyes from the Sun.

More Vocabulary

candle

A candle is something that is burned for light.

flashlight

A flashlight is a small lamp that uses batteries.

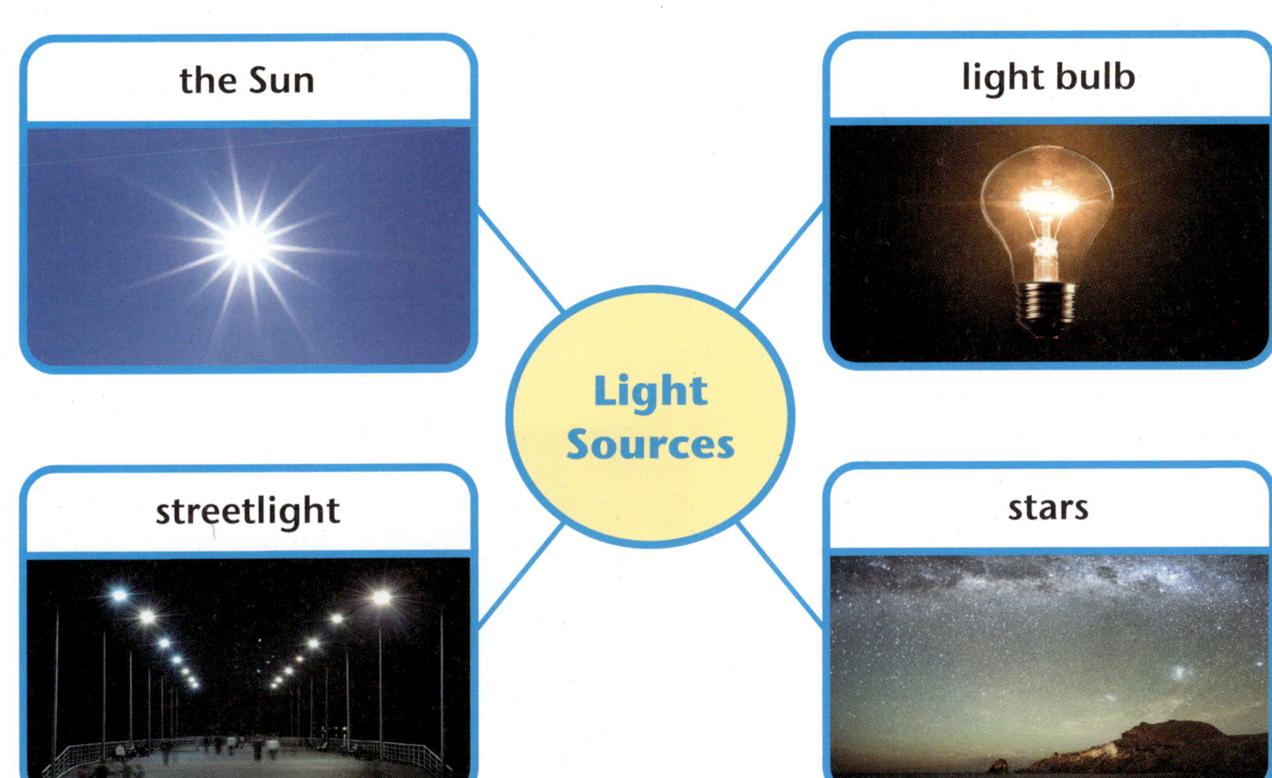

Up Close

Light and Shadow

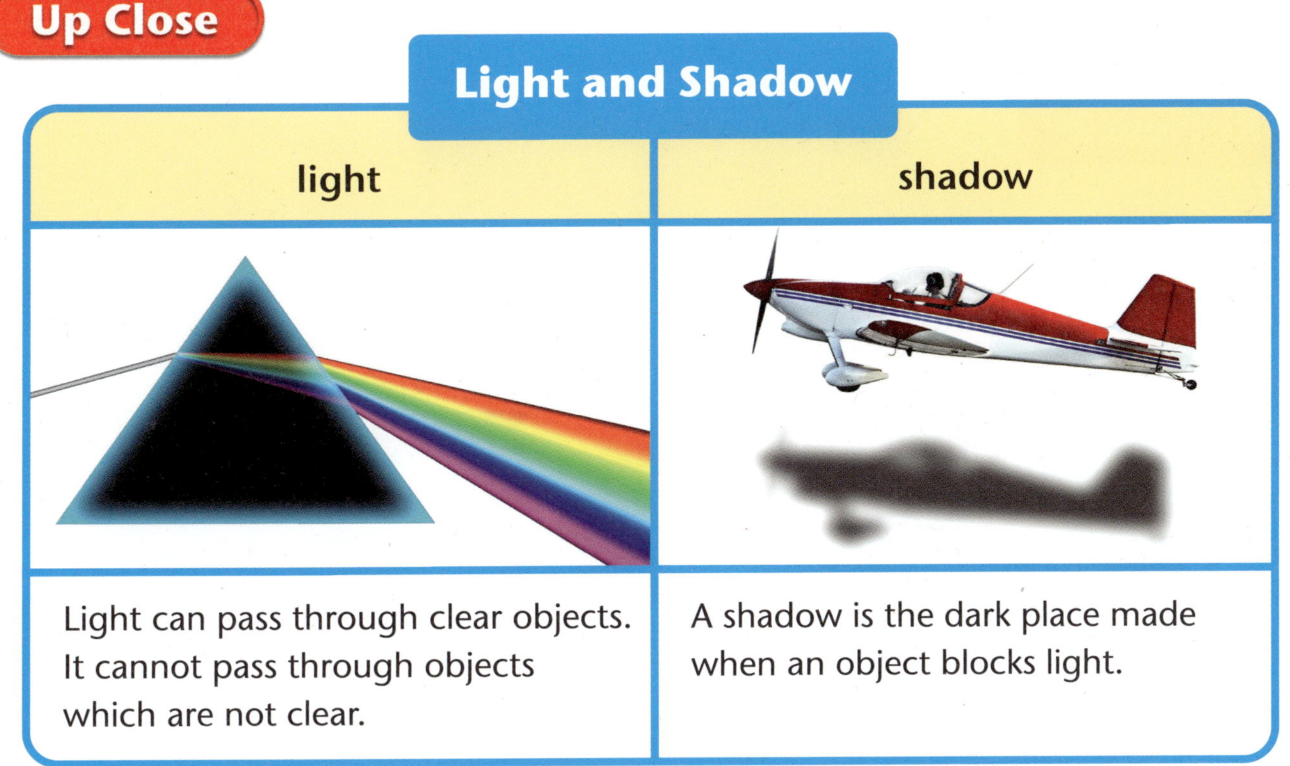

light	shadow
Light can pass through clear objects. It cannot pass through objects which are not clear.	A shadow is the dark place made when an object blocks light.

Match each word with the right picture.

1. shadow   ______
2. sunglasses   ______
3. light   ______
4. dark   ______
5. pass   ______
6. streetlight   ______

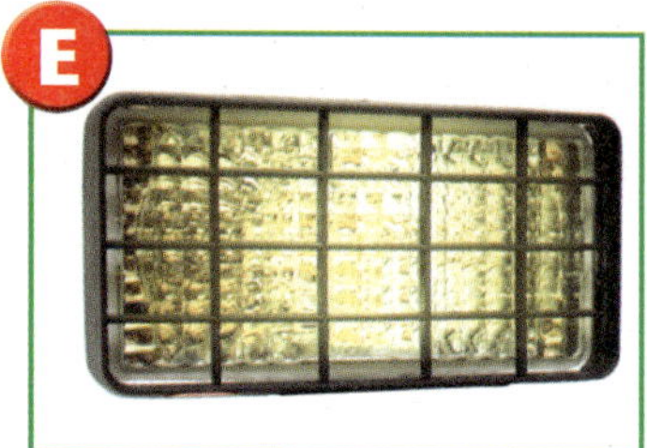

Choose the correct words.

1.

Sunlight (will / will not) pass through the plastic toy.

2.

Sunlight (will / will not) pass through the water.

Match each word with its definition.

1. the dark place made when an object blocks light

____

2. with no or very little light _______________

3. to go through _______________

4. a lamp on the street _______________

5. dark glasses that protect your eyes from the Sun

____

6. the energy that makes it possible to see things

____

shadow

sunglasses

light

dark

pass

streetlight

True or False

Circle T for true, F for false.

1. There is a lot of light in dark places.   T / F

2. Light makes it possible for us to see things.   T / F

3. A shadow is made when light passes through an object.   T / F

ATR-SC2-22
MP3

Read the passage. Complete the chart.

Light

Light is a kind of energy. Light comes from the sun. Light also comes from flashlights, candles and streetlights. Light is important because it lets us see things. Light can pass through clear objects. Light passes through clear glass or clear plastic. But light cannot pass through objects which are not clear. Sunglasses will block some light and protect your eyes. When you shine a flashlight on a toy, a dark shape of the toy will be formed. It is called a shadow. A shadow is made when an object blocks light. You can see many shadows on a sunny day.

READING SKILL Main Idea and Details

Light is a kind of energy.

Light comes from the sun, flashlights, candles, etc. Light lets us **A**____________.	Light **B**____________ through clear objects.	**C**____________ will block some light and protect your eyes.	A(n) **D**____________ is made when an object **E**____________ light.

Choose the correct answer.

1. What kinds of objects can light pass through?

   a. metal   **b.** people   **c.** glass

2. Light can come from things like ______________.

   a. shadows and the Sun
   b. candles and streetlights
   c. sunglasses and toys

3. Sunglasses will protect your eyes by ______________.

   a. letting all light from the Sun pass through it
   b. blocking some of the light from the Sun
   c. blocking all the light from the Sun

4. If you shine a flashlight on an object, ______________.

   a. you can see a dark shape of the object.
   b. the object will become clear.
   c. a shadow shaped like the flashlight is formed.

Critical Thinking

Write the correct answer.

1. Name three sources of light.

   ____

2. How can we see things at night?

   ____

Key Vocabulary

ATR-SC2-23
MP3

sound

Sound is the energy that you can hear.

vibrate

Vibrate means to move back and forth quickly.

pitch

Pitch is how high or low a sound is.

yell

Yell means to shout.

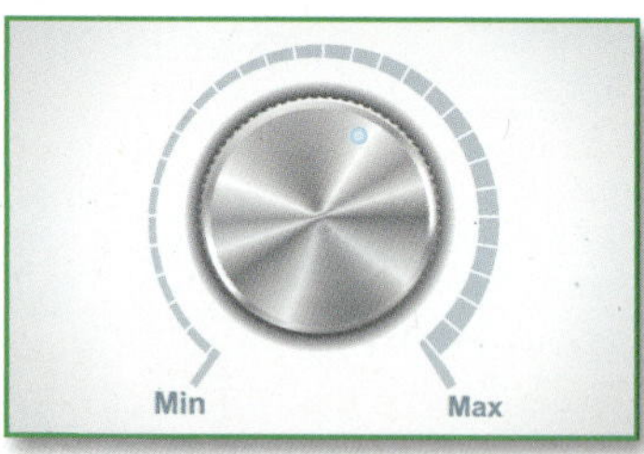

volume

Volume is how loud or soft a sound is.

whisper

Whisper means to speak quietly or softly.

More Vocabulary

drum
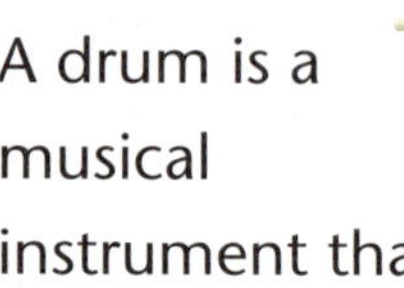
A drum is a musical instrument that you hit with your hands or a stick.

bell
A bell is a device that makes a ringing sound.

high
large in amount or degree

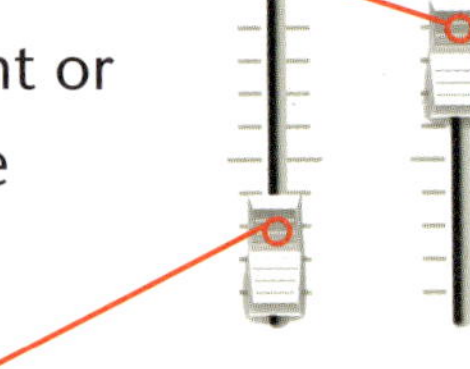

low
small in amount or degree

How do we hear sounds?

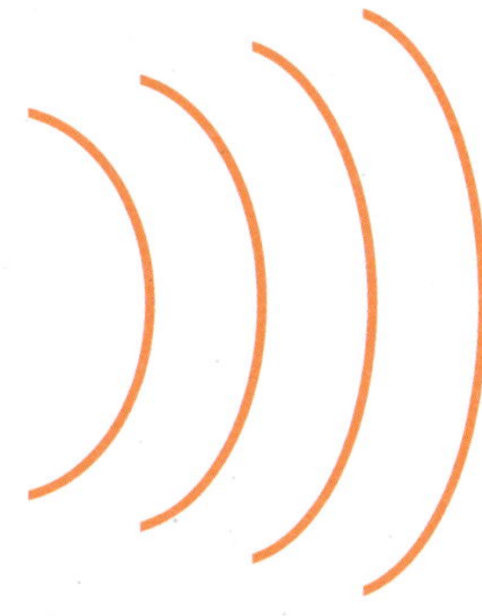

When you hit a drum, the drum vibrates.

The air around the drum vibrates too.

We hear the sound.

Up Close

Volume and Pitch

Volume is how loud or soft a sound is.

Pitch is how high or low a sound is.

Match each word with the right picture.

1. sound   _______
2. vibrate   _______
3. pitch   _______
4. volume   _______
5. yell   _______
6. whisper   _______

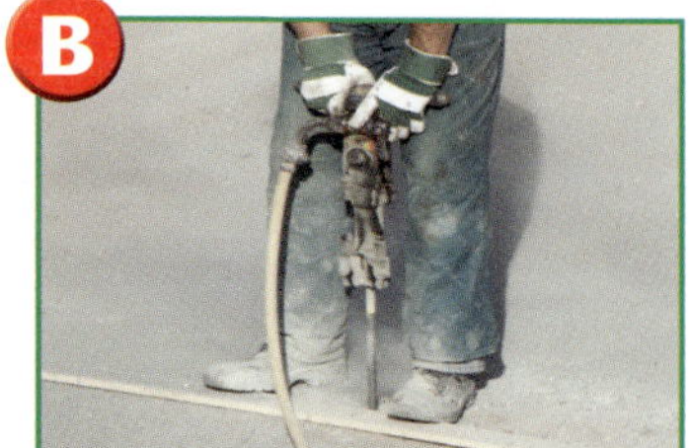

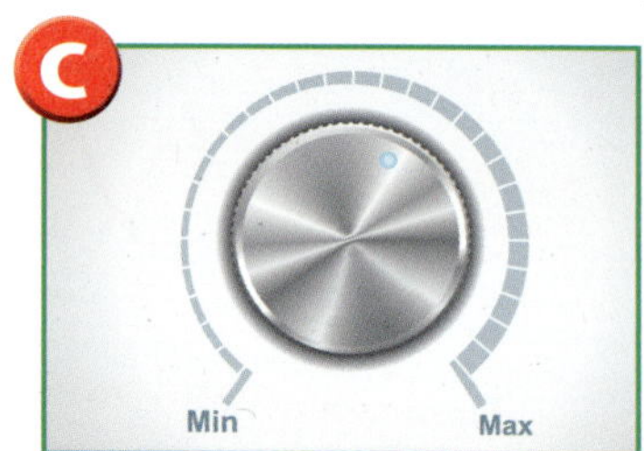

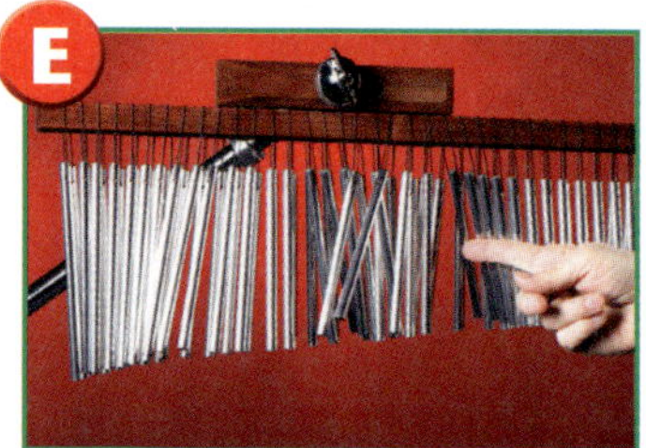

Choose the correct answer.

1. 
   a. loud sound
   b. soft sound

2. 
   a. high pitch
   b. low pitch

3. 
   a. high pitch
   b. low pitch

Match each word with its definition.

1. to move back and forth quickly

____

2. to speak quietly or softly ______________

3. the energy that you can hear

____

4. how high or low a sound is ______________

5. to shout ______________

6. how loud or soft a sound is ______________

> **volume**
>
> **yell**
>
> **sound**
>
> **whisper**
>
> **vibrate**
>
> **pitch**

True or False

Circle T for true, F for false.

1. Volume is how loud or soft a sound is.　　T / F

2. When you yell, you make a quiet sound.　　T / F

3. When you whisper, you make a quiet sound.　　T / F

ATR-SC2-24
MP3

Read the passage. Complete the chart.

Sound

Sound is a kind of energy that you can hear. Sound is made when something vibrates. Vibrate means to move back and forth quickly. When you talk or sing, place your hand on the side of your neck. Then you will feel your neck vibrating. When you hit a drum, it vibrates. Air around the drum vibrates

too. When the air reaches your ears, you hear the sound. There are loud sounds and soft sounds. The volume of a sound is how loud or soft a sound is. When you yell, you make a loud sound. When you whisper, you make a soft sound. All sound has pitch. Pitch is how high or low a sound is. A drum is an instrument with a low pitch. A bell is an instrument with a high pitch.

READING SKILL Compare and Contrast

Sound

ALIKE

Sound is made when something **A**______________.

DIFFERENT

B______________ of a sound is how
C______________ or soft a sound is.

D______________ of a sound is how high or low a sound is.

Choose the correct answer.

1. Sound is made when an object ____________.

    a. vibrates   **b.** hears   **c.** feels

2. A bell is an instrument with ____________.

    a. a low pitch   **b.** a high pitch   **c.** no pitch

3. When vibrating air reaches your ears, ____________.

    a. you hear a sound

    b. you see the sound

    c. the pitch is higher

4. If you do not want many people to hear you, ____________.

    a. you should yell loudly

    b. you should hit a drum

    c. you should whisper softly

Critical Thinking

Write the correct answer.

1. Can you name some things that make high-pitched sounds?

____

2. Which makes the louder sound when you yell or whisper?

____

Key Vocabulary

electricity

Electricity is energy that gives computers and other machines power to work.

ATR-SC2-25
MP3

power plant

A power plant is a building that produces electricity for many things or people.

fuel

Fuel is something burned to make heat or power.

battery

A battery is an object that stores electricity.

wire

A wire is a long, thin cable that carries electricity.

outlet

An outlet is a place on a wall for electricity.

More Vocabulary

cord

A cord is a cable used to connect machines to electricity.

dangerous

Dangerous means harmful and unsafe.

How Electricity Gets to Your Home

| Electricty comes from power plants through wires. | Electricity moves from the outlet through the cord. | Now the lamp has energy. Turn on the lamp. Then the lamp gives off light. |

Up Close

How do we use electricity at home?

| refrigerator | computer | stove | TV |

Match each word with the right picture.

1. electricity ______
2. outlet ______
3. fuel ______
4. wire ______
5. battery ______
6. power plant ______

A 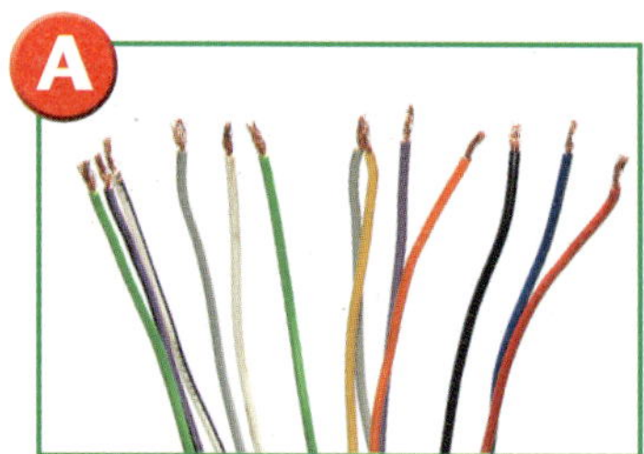

B 

C 

D 

E 

F 

Choose the things that use electricity to work.

1. 

a   b

2.  

a   b

Match each word with its definition.

1. energy that gives computers and other machines power to work _______________

2. a place on a wall for electricity _______________

3. a building that produces electricity for many things or people _______________

4. something burned to make heat or power _______________

5. a long, thin cable that carries electricity _______________

6. an object that stores electricity _______________

> outlet
>
> power plant
>
> battery
>
> fuel
>
> wire
>
> electricity

True or False

Circle T for true, F for false.

1. A power plant produces electricity. T / F

2. An outlet stores electricity. T / F

3. Wire is a cable that carries electricity. T / F

ATR-SC2-26
MP3

Read the passage. Complete the chart.

Electricity

Many things we use every day need energy to work. Electricity is a kind of energy. Electricity gives many things power to work. Power plants make electricity by burning fuel . Electricity moves through wires into buildings and homes. Electricity moves from the outlets to the machines through the cords . Electricity makes computers, lamps, refrigerators, TVs, and many machines work. Electricity makes streetlights shine. Sometimes machines get electricity from batteries . Electricity can run through water so never use it near water. Electricity can be dangerous .

READING SKILL Main Idea and Details

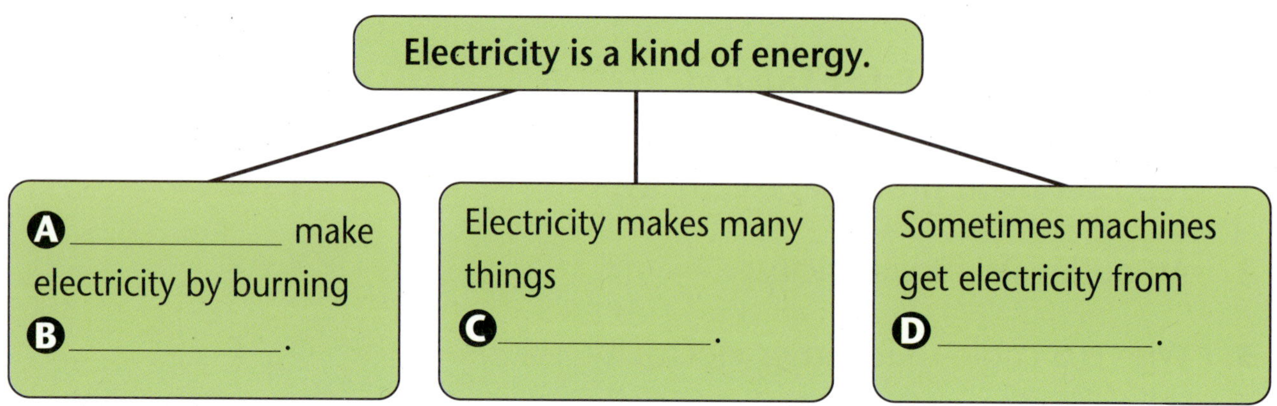

Choose the correct answer.

1. Electricity can run through water and can be _____________.
   a. burned   b. used   c. dangerous

2. Electricity moves _____________ to a machine through a cord.
   a. from an outlet   b. from a power plant   c. from a wire

3. Electricity is made in power plants, _____________.
   a. and is stored in fuel, wires, and cords
   b. and is made by burning machines
   c. and moves through wires into our homes

4. If you do not have electricity moving into your home, _____________.
   a. you can use a battery to get electricity
   b. you can burn fuel to make a battery
   c. you can burn fuel to make your computer work

Critical Thinking

Write the correct answer.

1. Can you think of some things that use electricity?

   ____

2. Can you think of some things that use batteries?

   ____

14 Motion

Key Vocabulary

ATR-SC2-27
MP3

motion

Motion is the act of moving.

speed

Speed is how fast something moves.

force

A power that produces a change in a movement. A push or a pull is a force.

gravity

Gravity is a force that pulls things to the ground.

pull

Pull is a force that moves things closer to you.

push

Push is a force that moves things away from you.

More Vocabulary

straight

Straight means not bent.

curved

Curved means not straight and forming a curve.

straight

curved

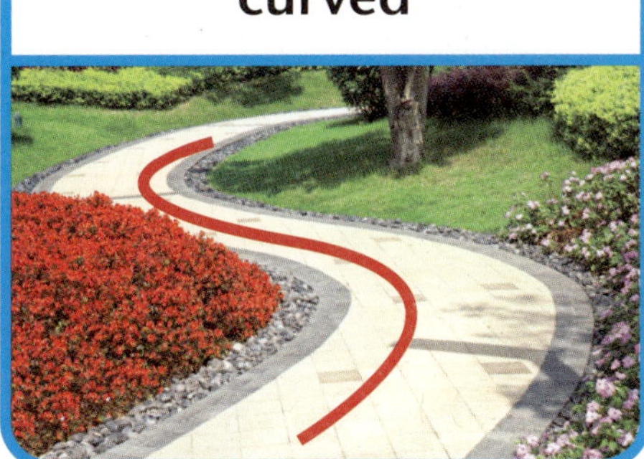

Changing Directions

circle

zigzag

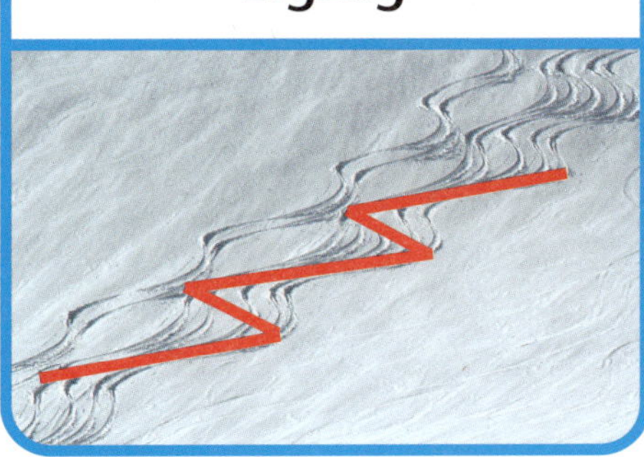

Up Close

Why do things fall?

Gravity is a force that pulls an object straight down to the ground.

Gravity keeps things from floating off into space.

Match each word with the right picture.

1. gravity ______
2. force ______
3. push ______
4. speed ______
5. motion ______
6. pull ______

Choose where each object will fall.

1   2

a   b   c   d   e   f

Match each word with its definition.

1. a force that moves things away from you

____

2. how fast something moves ______________

3. a force that moves things closer to you

____

4. a power that produces a change in a movement

____

5. a force that pulls things to the ground

____

6. the act of moving ______________

pull

motion

speed

push

force

gravity

True or False

Circle T for true, F for false.

1. Motion is where something is. **T / F**

2. A push or a pull is a force. **T / F**

3. A push is a force that moves things closer to you. **T / F**

ATR-SC2-28
MP3

Read the passage. Complete the chart.

Motion

If a car, person, animal, or other thing is in **motion**, it is moving. Things move at different **speeds**. A car moves fast, a person moves slowly. Things move in different ways. If you take the bus to school, you move quickly from your home to school. A train moves **straight**, but a train track can be **curved**. **Force** makes things move or stop. Force can change the speed of things. **Pushes** and **pulls** are forces. When you push an object, it moves away from you. When you pull an object it moves closer to you. A force that always pulls things down to the ground is **gravity**. When we drop an object, it falls because of gravity.

READING SKILL Cause and Effect

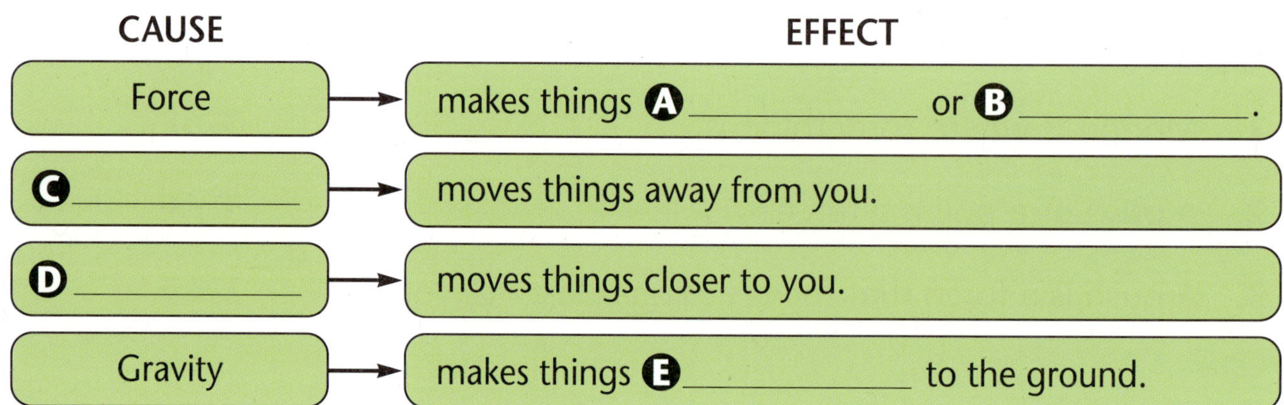

Choose the correct answer.

1. If something is in motion, then it is ______________.
    a. stopped   b. moving   c. straight

2. A force that always pulls things to the ground ______________.
    a. is called gravity   b. is called a push   c. is called motion

3. Objects can move at different ______________.
    a. speeds, but always move slowly
    b. speeds, but follow a curved track
    c. speeds and in different ways

4. When you push an object, it ______________.
    a. falls to the ground because of gravity
    b. moves away from your body
    c. moves slowly to the ground

Critical Thinking

Write the correct answer.

1. Why do things fall to the ground?

    ____

2. What will happen to us if there is no gravity?

    ____

15 Magnets

magnet

A magnet is a piece of metal that attracts iron or steel.

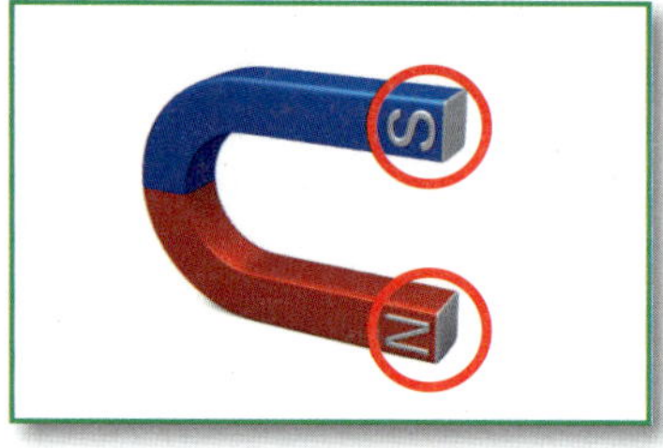

pole

A pole is one of the two ends of a magnet.

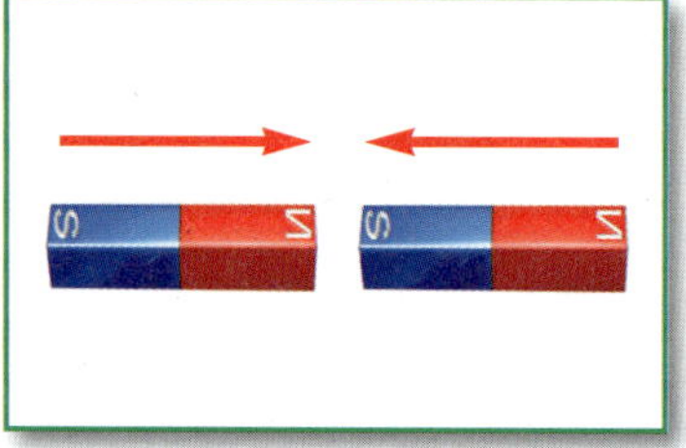

attract

Attract means to pull toward.

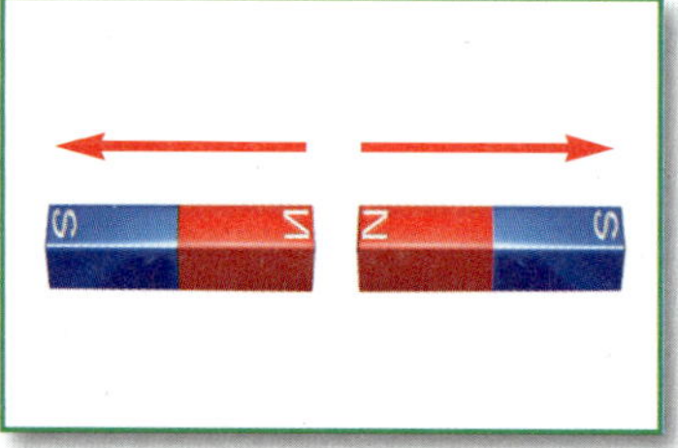

repel

Repel means to push away.

iron

Iron is a metal that is used to make many things.

steel

Steel is a kind of metal that is strong and has iron in it.

What do magnets attract?

attract		do not attract	
iron button		plastic button	
steel spoon		plastic spoon	
steel car		wooden car	

Poles of a Magnet

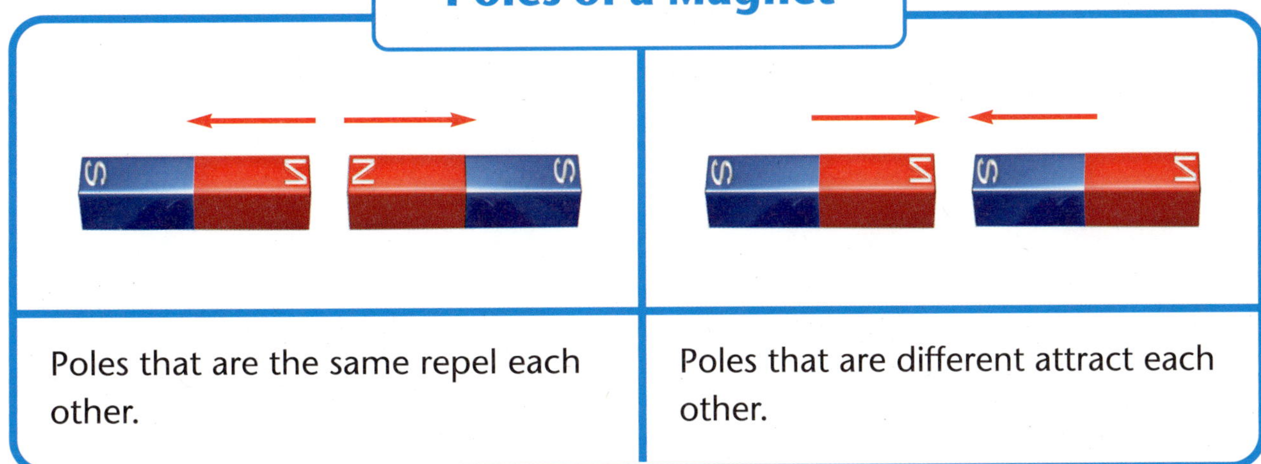

| Poles that are the same repel each other. | Poles that are different attract each other. |

Match each word with the right picture.

1. pole _______
2. attract _______
3. magnet _______
4. repel _______
5. iron _______
6. steel _______

A 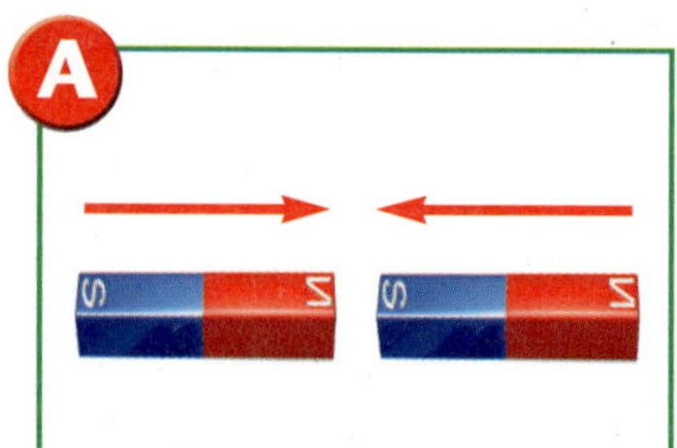

B 

C 

D 

E 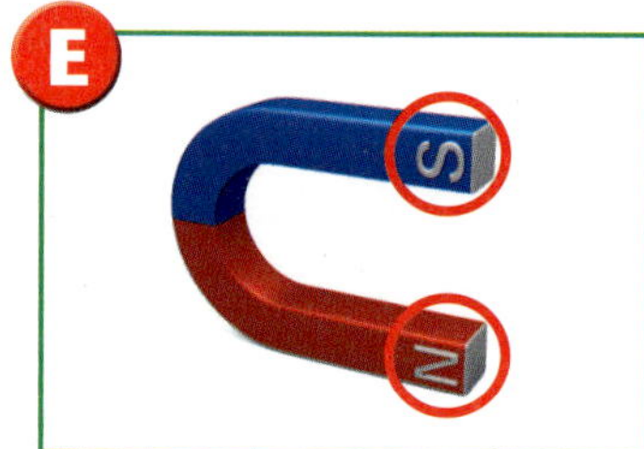

F 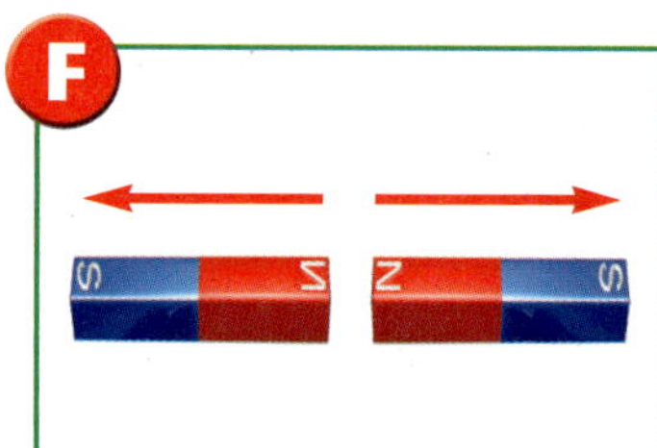

Choose the things that will be attracted to magnets.

a. 

b. 

c. 

d. 

Match each word with its definition.

1. to push away ________________

2. a strong metal that has iron in it ________________

3. a piece of metal that attracts iron or steel

____

4. one of the two ends of a magnet ________________

5. to pull toward ________________

6. a metal that is used to make many things

____

> pole
>
> attract
>
> magnet
>
> repel
>
> iron
>
> steel

True or False

Circle T for true, F for false.

1. A magnet is a piece of metal that attracts steel or iron.   **T / F**

2. Repel means to pull toward.   **T / F**

3. Steel is a metal that has iron in it.   **T / F**

ATR-SC2-30
MP3

Read the passage. Complete the chart.

Magnets

Magnets attract things made of iron.
Magnets attract things like paper clips
and steel spoons. They attract objects
without touching them. Magnets attract
metals that have iron in them. Magnets
do not attract things made of rubber,
wood, plastic, etc. Magnets have two
poles. The N shows the north pole and
the S shows the south pole. Try to put
two magnets together. If the poles are different, they will attract each
other. If the poles are the same, they will repel each other.

READING SKILL Details

Properties of a Magnet

Magnets do not
attract things made
of **A** ___________ ,
B ___________ ,
plastic, etc.

If you put together
two poles that are
different, they will
C ___________
each other.

If you put together
two poles that are the
same, they will
D ___________
each other.

Choose the correct answer.

1. Magnets will not attract things made of ____________.

   a. iron   **b.** plastic   **c.** magnets

2. Magnets can attract objects ____________.

   a. without touching them

   b. made from rubber

   c. but never repel objects

3. The same poles of a magnet will repel, but ____________.

   a. different poles will attract

   b. magnets cannot attract steel or iron

   c. different poles will also repel

4. Magnets will attract objects made of steel, because ____________.

   a. they have the same poles

   b. steel has iron in it

   c. steel attracts iron

Critical Thinking

Write the correct answer.

1. Which two metals do magnets attract?

____

2. What happens if two north poles are put together?

____

American Textbook Reading

Science ❷

Workbook

WorldCom Edu

American Textbook Reading

Science ②

Workbook

01 What Animals Need to Grow

1. Fill in the blanks using the words from the box.

1. shelter

2.

3.

4.

5.

6.

hatch   breathe   oxygen   store   nest   shelter

2. Choose the word that best completes the sentence.

1. Fish take _________ from the water.

a. hatch   b. shelter   c. oxygen   d. nest

2. The birds are carrying twigs to build their _________.

a. breathes   b. extincts   c. nests   d. protects

3. Dinosaurs are _________ animals.

a. need   b. shelter   c. breathe   d. extinct

4. The baby alligator __________ out of the eggs.

    a. hatches   **b.** oxygen   **c.** protects   **d.** nests

5. People need food, clothing and __________.

    a. hatch   **b.** shelter   **c.** extinct   **d.** nest

6. Animals need to keep their young safe, and __________ their young.

    a. extinct   **b.** breathe   **c.** oxygen   **d.** protect

Listen & Write

ATR-SC2-W31
MP3

Listen and fill in the blanks to complete the passage.

Animals need many things to live. First, animals need ❶ __________ to ❷ __________. Oxygen has no color and is made by plants. Second, animals need food to get energy. Some animals eat plants. Some animals eat other animals. And also there are animals that eat both plants and animals. Third, animals need to drink water to stay alive. Last, animals need ❸ __________. Shelters help to ❹ __________ animals from danger and keep them safe. For example, birds live in ❺ __________. They ❻ __________ their eggs in the nests and the eggs ❼ __________ in the nests. If animals do not have oxygen, food, water, and shelter, they could become ❽ __________.

02 Living Things vs Nonliving Things

1. **Fill in the blanks using the words from the box.**

1.

2.

3.

4.

5.

6.

> grow   survive   environment   rock   living things   nonliving things

2. **Choose the correct answer.**

1. Choose two things that are living things.

    a. a mammal   **b.** a rock   **c.** water   **d.** a bird

2. Choose two things that need food and water to survive.

    a. a reptile   **b.** an amphibian   **c.** ball   **d.** feather

3. If you eat food and get bigger, you will __________.

    a. nature   **b.** safe   **c.** rock   **d.** grow

4. Planting trees is very helpful for our __________.

    a. environment   **b.** safe   **c.** survive   **d.** nonliving thing

5. We can't __________ without food and water.

    a. survive   **b.** rock   **c.** environment   **d.** safe

6. Water is a __________.

    a. survive   **b.** rock   **c.** living thing   **d.** nonliving thing

Listen & Write

ATR-SC2-W32
MP3

Listen and fill in the blanks to complete the passage.

❶ _____________ has many living and nonliving things in it.

❷ _____________ need food and water to ❸ _____________. Food and water help living things to ❹ _____________ and change. Mammals, reptiles, birds, insects, amphibians, and fish are living things. People are living things too. The place where a living thing lives is called its ❺ _____________. A living thing must be ❻ _____________ in its environment. All living things are ❼ _____________. ❽ _____________ are not alive. Nonliving things do not need food or water, and do not grow. ❾ _____________ and water are nonliving things.

Vocabulary

1. Fill in the blanks using the words from the box.

1.

2.

3.

4.

5.

6.

> wild   spiny   adaptation   herbivore   camouflage   carnivore

2. Choose the word that best completes the sentence.

1. Tigers and lions are _________ that only eat meat.

    a. herbivores   **b.** carnivores   **c.** camouflage   **d.** adaptation

2. Deer and giraffes are _________ that only eat plants.

    a. herbivores   **b.** carnivores   **c.** camouflage   **d.** adaptation

3. I saw a(n) _________ dog in the forest.

    a. wild   **b.** herbivore   **c.** camouflage   **d.** adaptation

4. A _________ living thing has long sharp spikes for protection.

    a. color   **b.** spiny   **c.** carnivore   **d.** camouflage

5. A chameleon is the one of the _________ animals.

    a. shape   **b.** camouflage   **c.** food chain   **d.** spiny

6. Objects have different _________.

    a. wild   **b.** shapes   **c.** behavior   **d.** spiny

Listen & Write

ATR-SC2-W33
MP3

Listen and fill in the blanks to complete the passage.

Plants and animals have ❶ _____________ that help them survive.

An adaption is a body part or behavior that helps a living thing meet

its need. For example, some animals have spikes all around their

body which are very ❷ _____________ so that they protect

themselves from enemies. ❸ _____________ animals have adaptations.

❹ _____________ like tigers have sharp teeth for eating meat. Unlike

carnivores, ❺ _____________ have flat teeth for eating plants.

❻ _____________ is another adaptation. Camouflage is the color or

❼ _____________ of an animal that makes it blend in with its

environment. A chameleon can change the color of its body so that

it cannot be seen easily.

Vocabulary

1. **Fill in the blanks using the words from the box.**

1.

2.

3.

4.

5.

6.

| teen | child | infant | adult | sleep | toddler |

2. **Choose the word that best completes the sentence.**

1. ___________ makes your body strong.

a. Learn   b. Infant   c. Adult   d. Exercise

2. Your parents are ___________.

a. adults   b. exercises   c. infants   d. toddlers

3. They have one ___________, Sally. She is learning to walk and talk.

a. adult   b. toddler   c. teen   d. sleep

4. _________ can't walk or talk.

    a. Infants   **b.** Adults   **c.** Teens   **d.** Exercises

5. A(n) _________ starts to go to school.

    a. infant   **b.** toddler   **c.** sleep   **d.** child

6. _________ is as important as exercising.

    a. Adult   **b.** Child   **c.** Sleeping   **d.** Teen

Listen & Write

ATR-SC2-W34
MP3

Listen and fill in the blanks to complete the passage.

The life cycle of people is amazing. A person starts very small as an

❶ _____________. An infant cannot walk or talk. An infant grows into a

❷ _____________. A toddler starts to ❸ _____________ to walk and

talk. A toddler will grow into a ❹ _____________. A child can walk and

talk. Children begin to go to school and learn. When a person

becomes 13 years old, we call them a ❺ _____________. A teen is a

person between 13 and 19 years old. When a person becomes over 19

years old, we call them an ❻ _____________. An adult is a fully grown

person. During this cycle, we should be healthy. What is important

for being healthy? Every person should eat healthy foods and get

enough ❼ _____________ and ❽ _____________ to be strong and healthy.

Vocabulary

1. **Fill in the blanks using the words from the box.**

1.

2.

3.

4.

5.

6.

sunny	rainy	windy	weather	cloudy	snowy

2. **Choose the word that best completes the sentence.**

1. When snow turns to small pieces of ice, it is __________.

   a. wet   **b.** forecast   **c.** weather   **d.** sleet

2. This is good __________ for a walk.

   a. sleet   **b.** weather   **c.** observe   **d.** windy

3. From now, you should __________ it through sunglasses.

   a. observe   **b.** snowy   **c.** rainy   **d.** sleet

4. It rains a lot during the __________ season.

    a. sleet   **b.** rainy   **c.** snowy   **d.** observe

5. It is __________ today. Let's go play soccer!

    a. snowy   **b.** sunny   **c.** cloudy   **d.** wet

6. I don't like a(n) __________ day because I have to stay at home all day.

    a. wet   **b.** sleet   **c.** sunny   **d.** observe

Listen & Write

ATR-SC2-W35
MP3

Listen and fill in the blanks to complete the passage.

❶ ____________ is the conditions of the air outside. There are many different kinds of weather. It can be warm, cool, hot, or cold. You can ❷ ____________ how weather changes. Sometimes there is ❸ ____________ weather. On snowy days, the weather is very cold. Sometimes there is ❹ ____________. Sleet is a mix of snow and rain. On ❺ ____________ days, the weather is ❻ ____________. The rainy season occurs between June and July in some places. On ❼ ____________ days, you have to be careful of the wind. It might blow you away! When the weather is ❽ ____________, it could mean rain is coming. Sometimes the weather is beautiful and there is a lot of sun. This is called ❾ ____________ weather. It is good for people to play outside.

06 Measuring the Weather

Vocabulary

1. Fill in the blanks using the words from the box.

1.

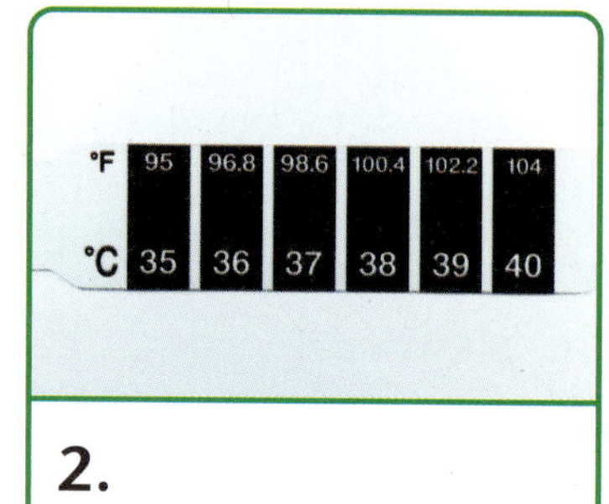

2.

3.

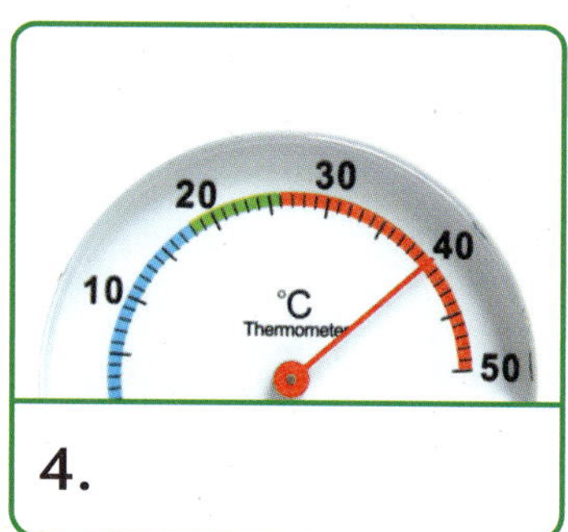

4.

5.

6.

| rain gauge | temperature | wind vane | thermometer | direction | measure |

2. Choose the word that best completes the sentence.

1. ___________ measures the amount of rain that falls.

    a. Wind vane   **b.** Rain gauge   **c.** Thermometer   **d.** Temperature

2. A ___________ measures the temperature of things.

    a. thermometer   **b.** rain gauge   **c.** measure   **d.** direction

3. She stood on the meter stick to ___________ her height.

    a. thermometer   **b.** heat   **c.** measure   **d.** tool

4. A scale is a __________ to measure one's weight.

    a. temperature   **b.** tool   **c.** measure   **d.** direction

5. __________ is a tool used to measure which direction the wind is blowing.

    a. Wind vane   **b.** Heat   **c.** Thermometer   **d.** Tool

6. The wind changed its __________.

    a. temperature   **b.** blow   **c.** wind vane   **d.** direction

Listen & Write

ATR-SC2-W36
MP3

Listen and fill in the blanks to complete the passage.

People can use ❶ ______________ to measure weather. Weather can be measured in many ways. One way to measure is to find the ❷ ______________ of the air. Temperature is the measure of how hot or cold something is. People can use a ❸ ______________ to measure the temperature of the air. People can also measure how much rain has fallen. A ❹ ______________ can be used to measure the amount of rain that has fallen. We can measure the direction and speed of wind. The ❺ ______________ the wind is ❻ ______________ can be measured by a ❼ ______________. A thermometer, rain gauge, and wind vane are all tools used to measure weather.

07 Clouds and Rain

1. Fill in the blanks using the words from the box.

1.

2.

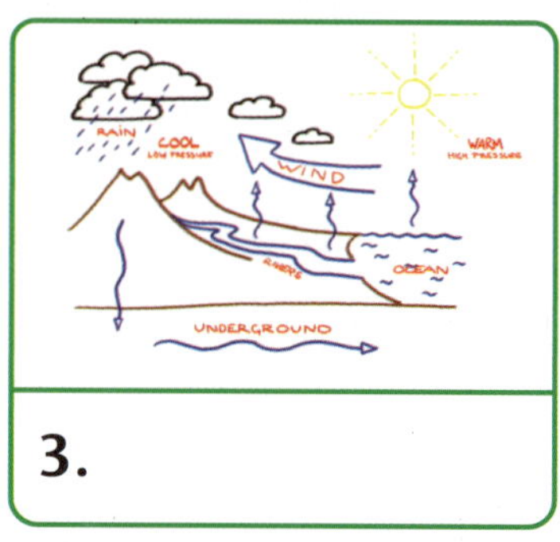

3.

4.

5.

6.

cycle	drop	condense	water vapor	cloud	evaporate

2. Choose the word that best completes the sentence.

1. Look at the dark __________. It is going to rain soon.

    a. cycle   **b.** clouds   **c.** water vapor   **d.** drops

2. __________ is water escaping in the form of vapor.

    a. Cloud   **b.** Drop   **c.** Water vapor   **d.** Cycle

3. Where is this sound of water __________ from?

    a. clouds   **b.** water vapor   **c.** drops   **d.** cycle

4. This dew is made by __________ vapor into water.

    a. condensing   **b.** disappearing   **c.** dropping   **d.** evaporating

5. Our four seasons is a __________ .

    a. drop   **b.** cloud   **c.** water vapor   **d.** cycle

6. When you __________ water, it changes into water vapor.

    a. condense   **b.** evaporate   **c.** cycle   **d.** drop

Listen & Write

ATR-SC2-W37
MP3

Listen and fill in the blanks to complete the passage.

Water moves from place to place. Water moves from the earth to the air and back again. This is called the water ❶ ______________. The Sun makes water warm. Then the water ❷ ______________, or changes into ❸ ______________. We cannot see water vapor. Water vapor goes up into the air. Water vapor cools in the sky. Then water vapor ❹ ______________, or changes into tiny water ❺ ______________. Many drops of water form ❻ ______________. Water drops in the clouds get bigger and bigger. They then fall back to the earth as rain or snow. The rain or snow falls into rivers, lakes and oceans. And the water cycle continues.

08 Seasons

1. Fill in the blanks using the words from the box.

1.

2.

3.

4.

5.

6.

| season | spring | summer | fall | winter | daylight |

2. Choose the word that best completes the sentence.

1. In __________, the weather is cold and snow falls.

    a. fall   **b.** summer   **c.** spring   **d.** winter

2. In __________, the weather is hot and we can enjoy ice cream every day.

    a. fall   **b.** summer   **c.** spring   **d.** winter

3. The weather becomes warmer and the plants begin to grow in __________.

    a. fall   **b.** summer   **c.** spring   **d.** winter

4. __________ is the season after summer. The weather is cooler.

    a. Fall   b. Summer   c. Spring   d. Winter

5. A __________ is a time of year. There are four different times of year.

    a. daylight   b. ripe   c. winter   d. season

6. In fall, many fruits are __________.

    a. ripe   b. daylight   c. fall   d. pattern

Listen & Write

ATR-SC2-W38
MP3

Listen and fill in the blanks to complete the passage.

A ① __________ is a time of year. There are four different seasons. Every season has different weather. The ② __________ of the seasons is always the same every year. ③ __________ is a warm and colorful season. There are many hours of ④ __________ in spring. We can play outside and enjoy the plant blossoms. In ⑤ __________, the weather is ⑥ __________ to spring but it becomes much hotter. Summer is a season for swimming at the beach. The weather becomes colder in ⑦ __________. There are less hours of daylight than in summer. Leaves change colors and drop from trees. Many fruits and vegetables are ⑧ __________ in fall. ⑨ __________ is the coldest season. In winter, snow falls and we have to wear our hats and gloves. Every season is different. There are special things to do in every season.

Vocabulary

1. Fill in the blanks using the words from the box.

1.

2.

3.

4.

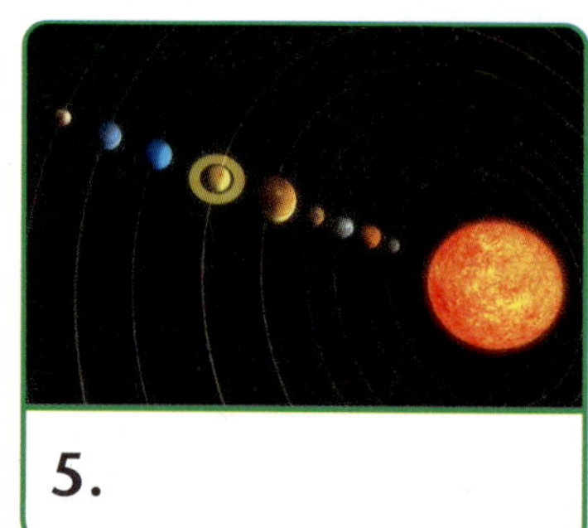

5.

6.

| sun | star | moon | planet | rotate | object |

2. Choose the word that best completes the sentence.

1. This box is full of rackets, balls and other __________.

   a. circles   **b.** rotates   **c.** objects   **d.** colors

2. No one knows how many __________ are in the universe.

   a. rotate   **b.** surface   **c.** circles   **d.** stars

3. The __________ moves around the earth.

   a. sun   **b.** rotate   **c.** moon   **d.** star

4. The __________ gives us daylight and warmth.

   a. circle   **b.** sun   **c.** moon   **d.** color

5. __________ have the names in our solar system.

   a. Planets   **b.** Suns   **c.** Rotates   **d.** Circles

6. The earth __________ like a top.

   a. plates   **b.** objects   **c.** rotates   **d.** moon

Listen & Write

ATR-SC2-W39
MP3

Listen and fill in the blanks to complete the passage.

Every day, the ❶ ______________ looks like it is moving across the sky. But actually the Sun is not moving. The sun looks like it is moving as the earth ❷ ______________. When the side we live on faces the Sun, we have day. When the side we live on turns away from the Sun, we have night. In the day sky, we can see the Sun. The Sun is a ❸ ______________. A star is an ❹ ______________ that makes its own light. The Sun gives light and warmth to the Earth. There's no sunlight in the night sky. In the night sky we can see ❺ ______________, stars and the ❻ ______________. Planets are objects that move around the Sun. The Earth is a planet. The moon is the object that move around the Earth. Planets, stars and the moon look small because they are far away from the Earth.

10 Heat

1. **Fill in the blanks using the words from the box.**

1.

2.

3.

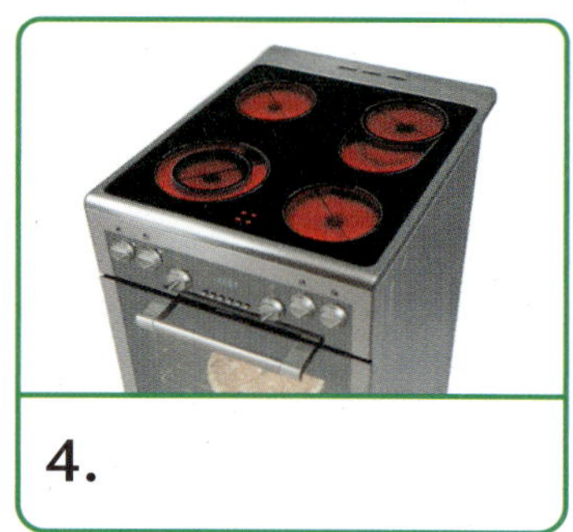

4.

5.

6.

| energy | warm | rub | heat | lamp | stove |

2. **Choose the word that best completes the sentence.**

1. Drinking hot milk can _________ you.

    a. stove   **b.** energy   **c.** warm   **d.** rub

2. Use a(n) _________ to see at night.

    a. lamp   **b.** heat   **c.** rub   **d.** stove

3. The dinner was on the _________.

    a. lamp   **b.** stove   **c.** rub   **d.** cook

4. If you ________ your hands together, it will warm them.

    a. stove   **b.** energy   **c.** lamp   **d.** rub

5. The Earth gets ________ from the Sun.

    a. stove   **b.** rub   **c.** heat   **d.** lamp

6. We eat food to get ________ to work and play.

    a. warm   **b.** energy   **c.** lamp   **d.** rub

Listen & Write

ATR-SC2-W40
MP3

Listen and fill in the blanks to complete the passage.

❶ ____________ is a kind of ❷ ____________. Heat, light, sound and electricity are forms of energy. Energy is something that makes things work or causes changes. Heat comes from many things. The Sun ❸ ____________ the Earth's land, water, and air. We get heat from burning things like wood or gas. ❹ ____________ produce light and also make heat. ❺ ____________ your hands together warms your hands. Heat is an important energy for us. Heat makes ice melt. Heat warms our body and our homes in winter. We also use heat to cook. We can cook food on a ❻ ____________.

11 Light

1. Fill in the blanks using the words from the box.

1.

2.

3.

4.

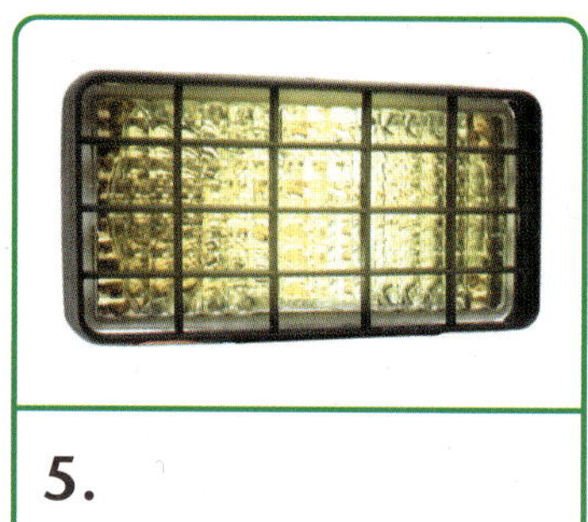

5.

6.

| shadow | sunglasses | light | dark | pass | streetlight |

2. Choose the word that best completes the sentence.

1. During the daytime, trees and buildings make __________.

    a. flashlights   **b.** shadows   **c.** candles   **d.** light

2. __________ protect our eyes from the sun.

    a. Sunglasses   **b.** Streetlights   **c.** Candles   **d.** Fireflies

3. We used __________ to see at night in the past.

    a. flashlights   **b.** streetlights   **c.** candles   **d.** shadows

4. Light __________ through a clear window.

    a. candles   **b.** darks   **c.** shadows   **d.** passes

5. When it is __________, we need a flashlight to see.

    a. streetlight   **b.** sunglasses   **c.** dark   **d.** light

6. __________ help us see at night.

    a. Streetlights   **b.** Sunglasses   **c.** Dark   **d.** Pass

Listen & Write

ATR-SC2-W41
MP3

Listen and fill in the blanks to complete the passage.

❶ ______________ is a kind of energy. Light comes from the sun. Light also comes from ❷ ______________, ❸ ______________ and ❹ ______________. Light is important because it lets us see things. Light can ❺ ______________ through clear objects. Light passes through clear glass or clear plastic. But light cannot pass through objects which are not clear. ❻ ______________ will block some light and protect your eyes. When you shine a flashlight on a toy, a ❼ ______________ shape of the toy will be formed. It is called a ❽ ______________. A shadow is made when an object blocks light. You can see many shadows on a sunny day.

12 Sound

1. Fill in the blanks using the words from the box.

1.

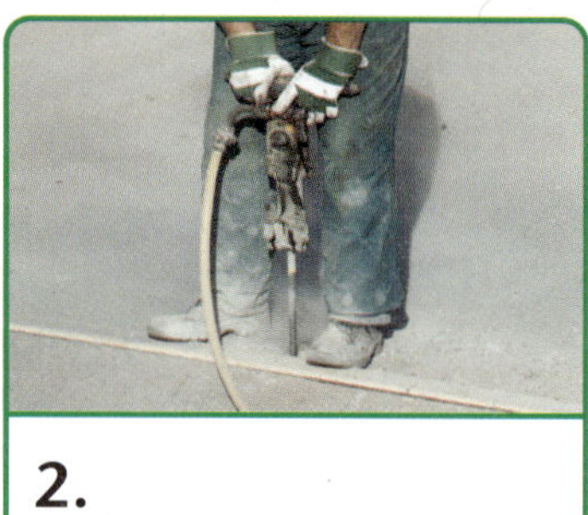

2.

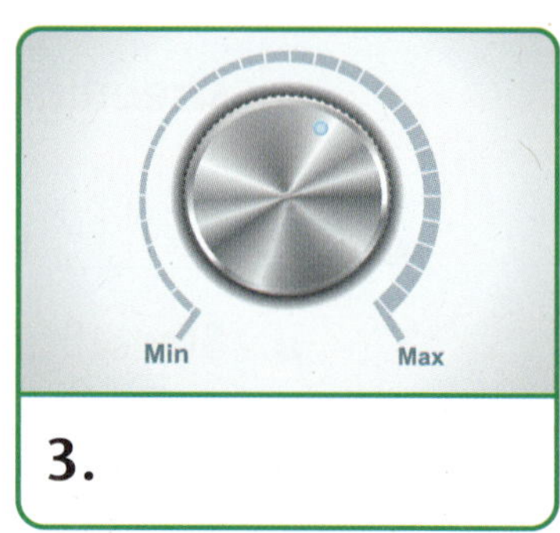

3.

4.

5.

6.

volume	yell	sound	whisper	vibrate	pitch

2. Choose the word that best completes the sentence.

1. My cell phone started to __________.

    a. pitch   **b.** drum   **c.** whisper   **d.** vibrate

2. The small bird has a high __________ sound.

    a. yell   **b.** pitch   **c.** whisper   **d.** drum

3. He __________ to her in the library.

    a. drum   **b.** yelled   **c.** whispered   **d.** pitched

4. The __________ of an ambulance warns us.

    a. drum   **b.** yell   **c.** sound   **d.** whisper

5. The TV is too loud. Please turn down the __________.

    a. volume   **b.** yell   **c.** whisper   **d.** vibrate

6. The little boy __________ to his friend.

    a. volume   **b.** vibrated   **c.** drum   **d.** yelled

Listen & Write

ATR-SC2-W42
MP3

Listen and fill in the blanks to complete the passage.

❶ __________ is a kind of energy that you can hear. Sound is made when something vibrates. Vibrate means to move back and forth quickly. When you talk or sing, place your hand on the side of your neck. Then you will feel your neck vibrating. When you hit a drum, it vibrates. Air around the drum vibrates too. When the air reaches your ears, you hear the sound. There are loud sounds and soft sounds. The **❷** __________ of a sound is how loud or soft a sound is. When you **❸** __________, you make a loud sound. When you **❹** __________, you make a soft sound. All sound has **❺** __________. Pitch is how **❻** __________ or **❼** __________ a sound is. A **❽** __________ is an instrument with a low pitch. A **❾** __________ is an instrument with a high pitch.

13 Electricity

1. Fill in the blanks using the words from the box.

1.

2.

3.

4.

5.

6.

> outlet   power plant   battery   fuel   wire   electricity

2. Choose the word that best completes the sentence.

1. There are _________ in the wall of my home.

    a. power plants   **b.** outlets   **c.** batteries   **d.** cords

2. You need a power _________ to use your computer.

    a. dangerous   **b.** fuel   **c.** electricity   **d.** cord

3. It is _________ to swim in deep water.

    a. fuel   **b.** electricity   **c.** dangerous   **d.** wire

4. __________ makes streetlights shine.

    a. Electricity   **b.** Dangerous   **c.** Cord   **d.** Outlet

5. My watch uses a __________ to make it run.

    a. power plant   **b.** fuel   **c.** dangerous   **d.** battery

6. Cars use gasoline as a(n) __________.

    a. fuel   **b.** electricity   **c.** battery   **d.** wire

Listen & Write

ATR-SC2-W43
MP3

Listen and fill in the blanks to complete the passage.

Many things we use every day need energy to work. ❶ __________ is a kind of energy. Electricity gives many things power to work.

❷ __________ make electricity by burning ❸ __________. Electricity moves through ❹ __________ into buildings and homes. Electricity moves from the ❺ __________ to the machines through the ❻ __________. Electricity makes computers, lamps, refrigerators, TVs, and many machines work. Electricity makes streetlights shine. Sometimes machines get electricity from ❼ __________. Electricity can run through water so never use it near water. Electricity can be ❽ __________.

14 Motion

1. **Fill in the blanks using the words from the box.**

1.

2.

3.

4.

5.

6.

| pull | motion | speed | push | force | gravity |

2. **Choose the word that best completes the sentence.**

1. The man started to walk in slow __________.

    a. gravity   **b.** straight   **c.** motion   **d.** pull

2. The racing cars are running at a fast __________.

    a. circle   **b.** pull   **c.** gravity   **d.** speed

3. __________ keep us on the ground.

    a. Curved   **b.** Gravity   **c.** Speed   **d.** Straight

4. I was __________ a cart around the grocery store.

    a. force   **b.** pushing   **c.** curved   **d.** gravity

5. She __________ the door open.

    a. curved   **b.** force   **c.** speed   **d.** pulled

6. Draw a __________ line instead of a curved line.

    a. gravity   **b.** pull   **c.** speed   **d.** straight

Listen & Write

ATR-SC2-W44
MP3

Listen and fill in the blanks to complete the passage.

If a car, person, animal, or other thing is in ❶ ______________, it is moving. Things move at different ❷ ______________. A car moves fast, a person moves slowly. Things move in different ways. If you take the bus to school, you move quickly from your home to school. A train moves ❸ ______________, but a train track can be ❹ ______________.

❺ ______________ makes things move or stop. Force can change the speed of things. ❻ ______________ and ❼ ______________ are forces. When you push an object, it moves away from you. When you pull an object it moves closer to you. A force that always pulls things down to the ground is ❽ ______________. When we drop an object, it falls because of gravity.

15 Magnets

1. Fill in the blanks using the words from the box.

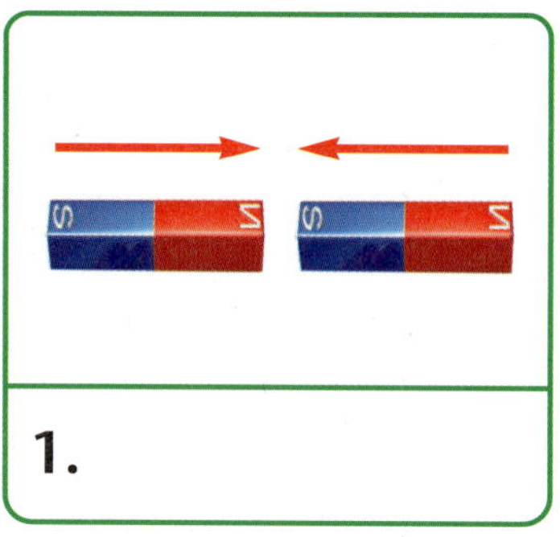

1.

2.

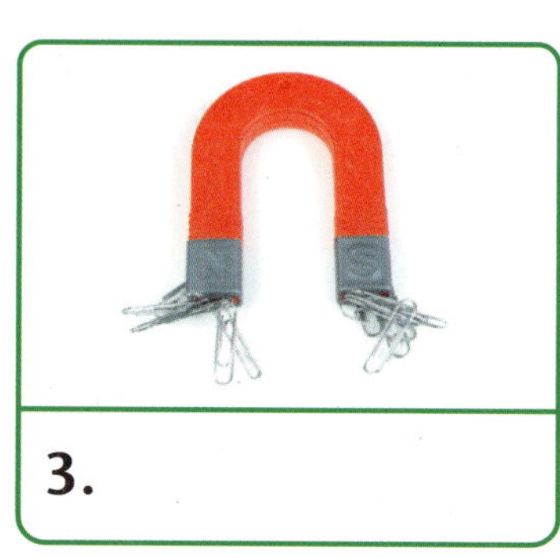

3.

4.

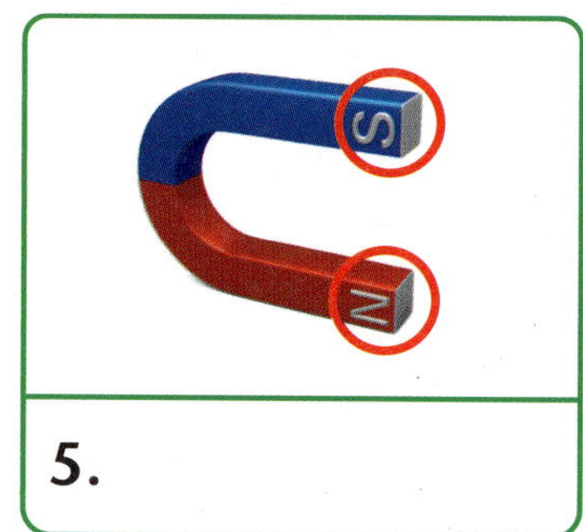

5.

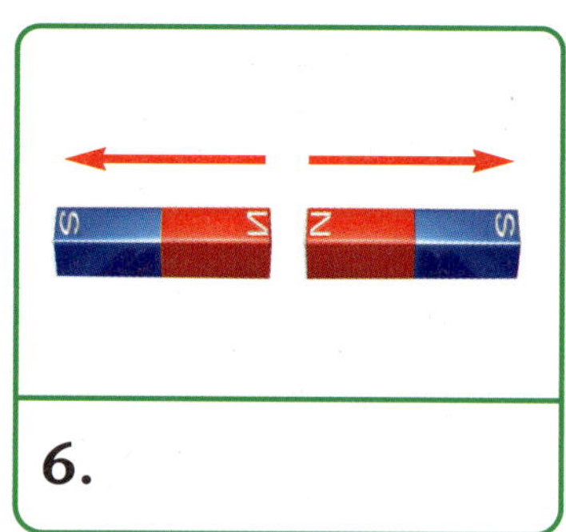

6.

| pole | attract | magnet | repel | iron | steel |

2. Choose the word that best completes the sentence.

1. A magnet has two __________.

   a. attracts   **b.** irons   **c.** steels   **d.** poles

2. A north pole and a south pole __________ each other.

   a. magnet   **b.** repel   **c.** attract   **d.** metal

3. Electricity travels through water and __________.

   a. plastic   **b.** steel   **c.** pole   **d.** attract

4. If you put two south poles next to each other, they will __________ one another.

    a. attract   **b.** metal   **c.** magnet   **d.** repel

5. __________ will not pull things like plastic or rubber.

    a. Magnets   **b.** Repels   **c.** Poles   **d.** Attracts

6. Paper clips have __________ in them.

    a. repel   **b.** iron   **c.** attract   **d.** magnet

Listen & Write

ATR-SC2-W45
MP3

Listen and fill in the blanks to complete the passage.

❶__________ ❷__________ things made of iron. Magnets attract things like paper clips and steel spoons. They attract objects without touching them. Magnets attract ❸__________ that have ❹__________ in them. Magnets do not attract things made of rubber, wood, plastic, etc. Magnets have two ❺__________. The N shows the north pole and the S shows the south pole. Try to put two magnets together. If the poles are different, they will attract each other. If the poles are the same, they will ❻__________ each other.

American Textbook Reading

Science ❷

WorldCom Edu   www.wcbooks.co.kr